ADAM HAMILTON

Enough
REVISED EDITION

Discovering Joy Through Simplicity and Generosity

Abingdon Press / Nashville

ENOUGH
Discovering Joy Through Simplicity and Generosity
Revised Edition

Library of Congress Cataloging-in-Publication Data has been requested.

This book is printed on elemental chlorine–free paper.
ISBN 978-1-5018-5788-1

18 19 20 21 22 23 24 25 26 27 — 10 9 8 7 6 5 4 3 2 1
MANUFACTURED IN THE UNITED STATES OF AMERICA

CONTENTS

THE COURAGE TO BE
FREE AND BEAR FRUIT

One of Jesus' great teaching parables involves a sower who cast seed along the ground. The sower hoped the seeds would sprout, grow, and bear good fruit. Some seeds did just that, producing a great harvest. But others, Jesus said, fell among thorns and, though they began to grow, these good plants were quickly choked out. Jesus said the thorns were "the cares of the world and the lure of wealth" (Matthew 13:22).

In a culture where having "enough" seems to have become a never-ending pursuit, Jesus' parable remains incredibly relevant. Many of us are chasing the American dream in ways that lead to stress, anxiety, and fear—thorns that can rob us of the ability to enjoy the abundant lives of purpose that God intended for us.

In America today, the average graduate leaves college owing more than $37,000 in student loan debt.[1] The average U.S. household carries credit card debt in excess of $16,000.[2] In 2014, the average Americans spent 25 percent of their income on housing.[3] In 2016 the average new-car loan was $30,032, with a payment of $503 per month; both amounts are record highs.[4] Among working-age families, the median amount that Americans have set aside for retirement is just $5,000.[5]

Given such numbers, it's not surprising that more than half of Americans are worried they won't be able to maintain their standard of living, and nearly two-thirds fear they won't have enough money for retirement.[6] It's little wonder that nearly half of Americans say they suffer from financial stress because their monthly expenses equal or exceed their income.[7] It's not difficult to understand why one of the leading causes of relationship stress and divorce is finances.[8]

This book is an invitation for you to rediscover truths, drawn from Scripture, that previous generations knew: We find joy and fulfillment in simplicity, relationships, a clear sense of purpose, generosity, and faith. These are the keys to experiencing the good life.

There is no sin in having wealth. Money itself is morally neutral. It can be used for good or evil. Much of the problem with wealth arises when we make the desire for more—more money and material possessions—a driving focus in our lives. That is the patch of thorns we must avoid.

The New Testament authors, writing in Greek, regularly used the word *metanoia*. The word is typically translated as "repentance." It literally means a change of thinking (values, ideals, understanding) that leads to a change of heart, and ultimately to a change in one's behavior.[9] My hope is that readers of this book, to the degree that we all struggle with a desire for more, will experience *metanoia*—we will see our material wealth with new eyes and come to be seized by the truth Jesus taught in Luke 12:15: "One's life does not consist in the abundance of possessions."

Paul wrote to the Corinthians that God is able to bless us with all that we need so that we "may share abundantly in every good work" (2 Corinthians 9:8). John Wesley, the founder of Methodism, echoed Paul's teaching when he urged Christians to make and save all they can through honest and honorable means—so they can give all they can.

When we choose to believe that life does not consist in the abundance of our possessions, but is found in relationships, in our faith, and in living purposeful lives, we become like the seed that fell on good soil. We become liberated to live the life that God intends for us.

CONTENTMENT PRAYER

Lord, help me be grateful for
what I have, remember that
I don't need most of what I want,
and that joy is found in simplicity
and generosity.

CHAPTER ONE

WHEN DREAMS BECOME NIGHTMARES

WHEN DREAMS
BECOME NIGHTMARES

Some people, eager for money, have wandered from
the faith and pierced themselves with many griefs.
1 Timothy 6:10b NIV

The lover of money will not be satisfied with money;
nor the lover of wealth, with gain. This also is vanity.
Ecclesiastes 5:10

"For what will it profit them if they gain the whole world but
forfeit their life? Or what will they give in return for their life?"
Matthew 16:26

Several years ago the Royal Bank of Scotland sent an offer for a Gold MasterCard to Monty Slater. The card came with a $20,000 credit limit—quite impressive for his first credit card, particularly when you consider that Monty is a Shih Tzu dog. Raymond, his owner, thought about using the card for some of Monty's favorite treats but reconsidered, recognizing that his pup was not in a position to pay the balance when it came due—and that might negatively affect Monty's credit rating![1]

This may be a funny story, but it illustrates a sobering truth: We live in a world that encourages us to live beyond our means. We are enticed to "have it now" and pay for it later, as opposed to saving and being good stewards of our God-given resources. We all are caught in the struggle in one way or another. No one is exempt—myself included.

For months I had been waiting for the new iPhone to arrive. I'd seen the commercials. I'd put my name on the list for more information. I had to have one. Then, two months before the phone was released, my Palm Treo phone broke, and the insurance I had purchased provided a brand-new one. I had a dilemma. I had a brand-new Treo, yet I wanted a new iPhone. I kept trying to convince myself that I needed a new iPhone, but I felt a twinge of guilt at the very thought because I had a brand-new phone. Finally, I decided I would wait until my new Palm Treo was a couple of years old and then buy an iPhone. *They will have perfected it by then, and it will be cheaper*, I told myself. It was settled.

It just so happened that the day the iPhone came out, I was out of town with the worship staff of our church. We had been visiting churches in another state and planning the sermons for the next year. That night we ate at a restaurant in an outdoor shopping mall and then decided to walk off our supper. As we walked, we came across an Apple store with a long line of people around it, each of them waiting to get an iPhone. I said, "Hey, I've got to go over there for a minute. I just have to see inside the store and look at the iPhone."

As we walked over to the store, someone came walking out with two new iPhones. I asked, "May I see one of your iPhones? I just want to hold the box. You don't even have to take it out." I just stood there holding the box in my hands and looking at it. Finally the staff said, "Hey, Adam, can we keep walking? Come on. Let's go."

"Okay," I said, "I'll be there in minute. Go ahead without me."

A few moments later I joined them, and we continued walking around the mall, eventually circling back to the Apple store. I walked up to the clerk at the door, whose job it was to let people in a few at a time, and I asked, "How late are you open tonight?"

He said, "We'll be open until midnight if there are any phones left by that time."

So we left, and we had our evening planning meetings. Around 11:30 that night, one of our staff members turned to me and said, "You want to go back there, don't you?"

I said, "Yeah, I really do."

"Come on; let's go," he said.

So we got in the car, drove back to the Apple store, and went inside. There was no line now, and they still had a handful of phones left.

I held the phone and had three different salesmen demonstrate its features for me. Before long I had convinced myself that I really needed it. I headed to the back of the store; yet all the while I was thinking to myself, *You have a new phone. Should you really be buying this?* I knew within a year the phone would come down in price. I knew I didn't need an iPhone. And I knew I wanted it now. I was torn.

By now it was 12:02 a.m. I thought to myself, *They were supposed to close at midnight, and these poor guys have been waiting on me; I'm obligated to buy it.* So I took the phone to the register and plunked down my credit card, still feeling a bit uncomfortable about the transaction. The strangest thing happened. For the first time in my life, my credit card was refused. I knew there was plenty of credit left on my account. The salesman asked, "Do you want to try another card?" I had another card in my wallet, but with a smile and a great sense of relief I said, "No, thanks anyway." It felt like a "God moment."

Now, I'm not suggesting that God has anything against iPhones, or that God goes around declining credit cards to save us from ourselves. It doesn't work that way. But this one time I had to wonder if God had intervened to make sure my credit card would not be approved!

I share this story to illustrate that we are a people who love stuff. We love gadgets and all the newest makes and models that come on the market. We want to replace our cars when they are only a few years old. We look in our closets overflowing with clothes and say we have nothing to wear because we want the newest fashion trends. We wrestle with these things.

Let me say that we must be very careful not to judge one another in this respect. We are in a position to judge only ourselves. We know how much money we make and how much we give away. We know how much we may need something or how much we may not. We know when it's okay to splurge and buy something we don't really need because there is balance in our lives, and we know when it's not okay. We know these things about ourselves; we do not know them about anyone else—even though we may think that we do.

> *"Do not judge, so that you may not be judged. For with the judgment you make you will be judged, and the measure you give will be the measure you get."*
> *(Matthew 7:1-2)*

There was a pastor who invited a missionary to speak at his church about social justice and ministry with the poor. As the pastor and missionary were pulling into the parking lot of the church, a man driving a brand-new, top-of-the-line Lexus drove in beside them. The missionary said, "Now that's what I'm talking about right there. I'm talking about those people driving cars like that." The pastor replied, "Let me straighten you out about one thing. I know this guy. He makes a million dollars a year. He gives $700,000 a year away to run the mission for the poor in our city. This guy is humble and caring. He could be driving a Rolls-Royce, but he lives five steps below his means. So don't criticize him. Would to God that you and I gave away as much of what we have as he does."

When it comes to material possessions and money, we are not in a position to pass judgment on others. We do not know how much they make and how much they give away. We do not know their hearts. All we can say is, "This is where I'm out of kilter; this is where I might need to change some things." So, throughout this chapter and the rest of this book, I invite you to focus on what God may be speaking to you, rather than to pass judgment on anyone else.

Now, before we are able to address the solution to our desire for more, we must better understand the problem itself. Let us begin by considering the American Dream.

THE AMERICAN DREAM

What is the "American Dream"? To be sure, there have been some lofty dreams in our nation's history. Our founders had a dream about life, liberty, and the pursuit of happiness. There was the dream of freedom and new beginnings so beautifully expressed in the inscription on the inside of the pedestal of the Statue of Liberty: "Give me your tired, your poor, your huddled masses yearning to breathe free. . . ." There also was the dream of equality and opportunity conveyed in Dr. Martin Luther King Jr.'s famous "I Have a Dream" speech. These are all lofty dreams, but they generally are not what people mean when they talk about the "American Dream." For most people, the American Dream has to do with a subconscious desire for achieving success and satisfying the desire for material possessions. It is the opportunity to pursue more than what we have, to gain more than what we have, and to meet success. And we tend to measure our success by the stuff that we possess.

Alexis de Tocqueville, a political philosopher who came to America in the nineteenth century, made this observation:

> [Americans] are extremely eager in the pursuit of immediate material pleasures and are always discontented with the position that they occupy. . . . They think about nothing but ways of changing their lot and bettering it. For people in this frame of mind every new way of getting wealth more quickly, every machine which lessens work, every means of diminishing the cost of production, every invention which makes pleasures easier or greater, seems the most magnificent accomplishment of the human

mind....One usually finds that the love of money is either the chief or a secondary motive at the bottom of everything the Americans do. This gives a family likeness to all their passions and soon makes them wearisome to contemplate.[2]

To be sure, we are eager in the pursuit of immediate material pleasures. The love of money and the things money can buy is indeed a primary or secondary motive behind most of what we do. Consuming, acquiring, buying—this is what the American Dream has come to mean. Thus, what is commonly understood as the "American Dream" might more accurately be called the American nightmare.

THE AMERICAN NIGHTMARE

How did the "American Dream" become a nightmare? To a great extent, it is due to two distinct yet related illnesses that affect us both socially and spiritually.

Affluenza

The first illness is called *affluenza*, which is the constant need for more and bigger and better stuff—as well as the effect that this need has on us. A program on the local station of the Public Broadcasting Service defined affluenza this way:

affluenza, n. 1. The bloated, sluggish, and unfulfilled feeling that results from efforts to keep up with the Joneses. 2. An epidemic of stress, overwork, waste, and indebtedness caused by dogged pursuit of the American Dream. 3. An unsustainable addiction to economic growth.[3]

Most of us have been infected by this virus to some degree. If we're honest, we all must admit that we've struggled at one time or another with the desire to acquire.

It's no secret that shopping is one of Americans' favorite pastimes. Shopping has become an American way of life. Our economy is dependent upon consumer spending, which is why we measure it and report it on the nightly news. We tune in to hear about the impact of consumer spending on the stock market and on our retirement funds. We're even told that our spending determines the strength of our nation. There's some logic to all of this, but somehow it tends to fuel the illness that's inside of us. And there are whole marketing plans to fuel that illness.

Every newspaper we pick up and every television show we watch is filled with advertisements for which someone paid thousands—or even millions—of dollars in the hope of convincing us that we need something else. And they're good at it! The voices whisper in our heads, fueling something that's already inside us, and we find ourselves thinking, That's right. I do need that. No doubt you can quickly think of something you hope to purchase next—new clothes, a new computer, new furniture, a new car, a new kitchen, a new house. We all sense the continuous fueling of our desire for more. And yet we do not have room for all the stuff we already have.

An article on Slate.com noted that according to the National Homebuilders Association, the average American home went from 1,660 square feet in 1973[4] to nearly 2,700 square feet in 2016[5]—yet we still have to rent storage space to hold all of our things. Self-storage space in America is continually increasing, and today there is estimated to be 2.3 billion square feet of self-storage space.[6] An entire market has developed for storing the stuff we're enticed to buy—often with money we do not actually have.

Credit-itis

This brings us to the second disease that goes along with affluenza: *credit-itis*. Credit-itis is the opportunity for us to buy now and pay later. It's an illness that is brought on by promises of "six months same as cash," or a 20 percent discount if you use your store credit card. It's basically the idea that you can enjoy something today and pay for it tomorrow, and it feeds on our desire for instant gratification. Our economy today is built on the concept of credit-itis. Unfortunately, it has exploited our lack of self-discipline and allowed us to feed our affluenza, wreaking havoc in our personal and national finances.

It didn't used to be that way. When I was growing up, my mom would take us kids every August to the department store to try on our fall and winter clothing, including our winter coats. We would say, "Why are we trying on coats? It's hot outside." And she would insist that we had to do it. So we would try on the clothes, and then Mom would put them on layaway. I remember that it was usually so cold outside that we could hardly stand it when Mom would finally make the last payment on the coats. Then and only then could we get the coats out of layaway and wear them.

Kids today don't know what layaway is. What an odd idea—to save up the money and make payments and be able to take the items home only after paying for them in full. But that's how it worked.

Today, credit cards have replaced layaway, and more and more Americans are going deeper and deeper in debt in order to have what they want now and pay for it later. According to a popular advertising slogan, "There are some things money can't buy, but for everything else, there's MasterCard." Average credit card debt in America in 1990 was around $3,000. Today, it's close to $17,000.[7] Considering that many Americans pay off their credit cards each month, the average debt for those who maintain a balance must be significantly higher than that figure. Some people actually move sums from one credit card to another, which means that the figure might be higher still.

It used to be that credit card companies required you to make a 4 percent minimum payment on your credit card balance. Today, many credit card companies allow you to make a 2 percent minimum payment; some will allow you to pay as little as 1 percent.[8] Assuming that you have a balance of $9,000 on your credit card and you never use the card again, it would take approximately 240 years to pay off your existing balance making a 2 percent payment each month while paying 18 percent annual interest. In other words, you would never pay it off making minimum payments.

It makes it even more difficult to pay down a credit card balance when we continue to buy things we never would have bought if we had to reach into our billfolds and take out cash. The average sale is around 125 percent higher if we use a credit card than if we pay cash, because we're not thinking about the money when we use credit. It doesn't feel real when we use plastic instead of cash.

Unfortunately, credit-itis is not limited to purchases made with credit cards; it extends to car loans, mortgages, and other loans as well. Let's look first at car loans.

A 2006 survey showed that 89 percent of new car buyers were financing their vehicles for over four years and that 55 percent were choosing loans that extended more than five years.[9] By 2017, the average car loan had reached a record length of 69 months.[10] When I investigated online to see how many months I could finance a new $30,000 car, I found thousands of websites that offered me a 96-month loan—that's eight years. If I average 15,000 miles a year, that $30,000 car will have 120,000 miles on it by the time I finish paying it off.

Of course, few people keep a car for eight years anymore. The average is three to four years. So, when I go to trade in that car, I discover that I'm driving "upside down"—I owe more than the car is worth. But the car dealer can help me with that by rolling the difference into a new car loan. Now, without paying anything down, I can finance 105 percent of the purchase price of the new car. Then, three years later when I want to trade in that car, the car dealer will roll in the difference once more so that I'm financing 110 percent of the purchase price. Before long I have become an indentured servant of the car finance company! Many of us buy cars in this manner, shopping for monthly payments rather than thinking about the purchase price of the vehicle and the total interest to be paid. We just don't stop to think about the long-term consequences of what we're doing.

The same trend can be seen in home mortgages. Traditionally, the life of a home mortgage has been either fifteen or thirty years, with 5 percent down. Now, many mortgage lenders are offering forty-year mortgages, and some even offer a fifty- or sixty-year mortgage. There are interest-only mortgages and adjustable-rate mortgages, which enable people to buy homes they otherwise could not afford. And in recent years, many people have taken out two mortgages—one for

80 percent and the second for 20 percent, plus the closing costs—so that they may get into the homes they want with nothing down and no Private Mortgage Insurance (PMI) required. Prior to the recent economic crisis, even people with poor credit were able to borrow money in order to buy homes with little or nothing as a down payment. These loans are known as "subprime" loans because the borrowers were not "prime" borrowers.

In addition to home mortgages, the last few years have seen a boom in home equity loans, which allow us to withdraw the money from what is, for most of us, our single largest savings account—removing the equity from our home and spending it. So instead of paying down the mortgages on our homes, many of us choose to withdraw the equity for home improvements or other purchases. Recently, I received an offer from my mortgage lender to loan me more than I paid for my house eight years ago—and my house is not close to being paid off. That's a lot of extra cash I could spend on anything I wanted. No new appraisal. No closing costs. No need to show bank statements or verify other assets. No paycheck stubs or proof of income required. I was told I could take out all the equity in my home—and quite a bit more. If I actually took out this loan, you would have to visit me in jail because the amount of money they offered was more than I could reasonably pay back.

It's these kinds of offers that feed our desire to have it now and pay later. They entice us to take out all the equity in our homes, which should continue building up over time, and spend it on stuff. I don't know about you, but I don't want to pay for eating out for the next thirty years on my mortgage.

Another problem related to the illness of credit-itis is the issue of declining savings. As late as 1982, the savings rate for Americans was at 10 percent.[11] Thirty-five years later, in 2017, this number was just 5.7 percent.[12]

Even college students are contributing to the problem. The average student graduates with $37,000 in student loans, but most who take out student loans have far more debt than that.[13] Students are now using these loans not only for tuition but also for cars, iPhones, clothes, and other items. What's more, the average college student has more than $3,000 in credit card debt when he or she graduates.[14] I could go on and on with statistics such as these, but the point is this: We have become a credit-crazed society. Even those of us who are not in debt up to our ears know that most Americans spend money with very little self-discipline. We look at our W-2 at the end of the year and wonder, "Where did it all go?"

This is the American nightmare, and it leads to debt collectors and personal bankruptcy—not to mention tremendous stress. In his book *Priceless*, Dave Ramsey reports the sobering fact that "the number one cause of divorce is financial issues."[15] We are suffering the consequences of our addiction to consumption and compulsive buying, and yet our desire for more is never satisfied. This is because there is a deeper problem—one that is within us.

> *"But strive first for the kingdom of God and his righteousness, and all these things will be given to you as well." (Matthew 6:33)*

THE DEEPER PROBLEM WITHIN

There is a spiritual issue that lies beneath the surface of affluenza and credit-itis. This issue is not new; it has been a part of humanity almost from the beginning.

Inside us there is a brokenness; the Bible calls it sin. Our souls were created in the image of God, but they have been distorted. We were meant to desire God, but we have turned that desire toward possessions. We were meant to find our security in God, but we find it in amassing wealth. We were meant to love people, but instead we compete with them. We were meant to enjoy the simple pleasures of life, but we busy ourselves with pursuing money and things. We were meant to be generous and to share with those in need, but we selfishly hoard our resources for ourselves. There is a sin nature within us.

Three of the seven deadly sins relate directly to the problem we have with money and possessions. First, we are afflicted by envy or covetousness. We want what others have, and we will do whatever we can to get it—whether that means taking it or buying it for ourselves. Second, we are afflicted by greed or avarice. We have an intense desire for more and don't want to share what we have. And third, we are afflicted with gluttony. We keep consuming, even when we are full and our needs are met—and we finally make ourselves sick.

I was taken by the comments of Craig Gay, who wrote, "The most serious indictment we must level at contemporary consumer behavior is that it is 'spiritless.' It betrays a decision to sacrifice all noble and truly human aspirations at the altars of comfort, convenience, and safety."[16] I would add "pleasure" to that list of altars. We are living lives without meaning, and we are slaves to sin. That is what's wrong with us. I'm not suggesting that all consumption is wrong—only that we've taken something meant to be enjoyed in one way and made it the central focus of our lives. We have surrendered to the sin nature within us.

> *"The thief comes only to steal and kill and destroy. I came that they may have life, and have it abundantly." (John 10:10)*

I find that the devil plays upon this sin nature. Whether we see the devil as a literal figure or the personification of the force that tempts us and moves us away from God's will, we read in the Scriptures that the devil tempts us and plays upon these weaknesses in our souls. His delight is to undermine our effectiveness as Christ's people, replacing our joy with misery.

Jesus said, "The thief comes only to steal and kill and destroy. I came that they may have life, and have it abundantly" (John 10:10). The devil doesn't need to tempt you to do drugs or to steal or to have an extramarital affair in order to destroy you. All he needs to do is convince you to keep pursuing the American Dream—to keep up with the Joneses, borrow against your future, enjoy more than you can afford in the present, and indulge yourself. And by doing that, he will rob you of joy, make you a slave, and keep you from doing God's will.

When I think of the ways the devil tempts us regarding greed, I think of the last temptation of Christ in Matthew's Gospel. The devil took Jesus to where he could picture all of the riches and glory of the world, and he offered it to Jesus if Jesus would only choose to turn away from God's path (see Matthew 4:8-10). Jesus was literally tempted to pursue wealth and power as opposed to sacrificial love. If Jesus was tempted in that way, certainly we can count on being tempted in that way.

Here's what the devil knows: If he can get you in debt, he can make you a slave. If he can convince you to spend all you have, you'll never offer your tithes to God, never help the poor as you could have, and never use what you do have to accomplish God's purposes. If he can tempt you to become a slave to creditors, you will not know simplicity, generosity, or joy. He will have neutralized your effectiveness for the Kingdom and choked the gospel out of your life.

That's what Jesus was saying in the parable of the sower and the soils. He told about a farmer who sowed seed, and some of the seed fell among the thorns and weeds. Jesus described the result this way: "As for what fell among the thorns, these are the ones who hear [the word of God]; but as they go on their way, they are choked by the cares and riches and pleasures of life, and their fruit does not mature" (Luke 8:14). That's what happens to us when we are afflicted with affluenza and credit-itis. Too much of our energy and our thoughts and our heart's desire go into acquisition and pleasure, and there's nothing left to nurture the fruit God intends us to produce. Our spiritual lives remain immature and unfruitful as long as we're pursuing the American Dream dictated by our culture.

> *"What does it profit a man to gain the*
> *whole world, and forfeit his soul?"*
> *(Mark 8:36 NASB)*

We're not thinking about the things of God while the creditors are calling. We can't experience the blessing and the joy that come from giving freely to things that matter when we can't make ends meet. We can't even "be still, and know that [he is] God" (Psalm 46:10) because we've got too many gadgets we're listening to.

Jesus said it this way: "What does it profit a man to gain the whole world, and forfeit his soul?" (Mark 8:36 NASB). Similarly, Paul described what happens to many of us when he wrote to Timothy, "Some people, eager for money, have wandered from the faith and pierced themselves with many griefs" (1 Timothy 6:10b NIV).

THE BIBLE'S SOLUTION

So, what is the answer? In the following chapters we will look at biblical teachings and practical tips related to how we can change our habits, get out of debt, get a handle on our money and possessions, live more simply, and give more generously. But before we consider these things, we must acknowledge that the starting point is a healing transformation in our hearts. We need a changed heart, which results in changed desires and a changed sense of our life purpose. And here's the good news: This is something God specializes in!

Although I accepted Christ and received a changed heart years ago, I find that, in a sense, I need a heart change every morning. So, each morning I get down on my knees and say, "Lord, help me be the person you want me to be today. Take away the desires that shouldn't be there, and help me be single-minded in my focus and my pursuit of you." As I do this, God's Spirit works to change me from the inside out, purifying my heart.

One day in a chapel service, some members of my church staff offered a wonderful and compelling illustration of how God works within us. They noted that in some ways human beings are like a pumpkin that is to become a jack-o'-lantern. If you've ever picked pumpkins from the field, you know that no pumpkin is perfect. The task is to incorporate your pumpkin's imperfections into the design you carve into it. You look at the pumpkin and begin to imagine what it can be. Next, you draw on it a face of some sort. Then you come to the first step in the actual transformation of the pumpkin, which also is the messiest. You open it up, and you begin to scoop out all the nasty, slimy, smelly stuff inside. Then you carve the face or design, which is no doubt a bit painful for the pumpkin. And, ultimately, you replace all of the muck with a light that shines from within.

This is a picture of what God intends: that greed and envy and materialism have been replaced, and that God's light shines within us in a way that gives light to others.

As we allow Christ to work in us, seeking first his kingdom and striving to do his will, we begin to sense a higher calling— a calling to simplicity and faithfulness and generosity. We begin to look at ways we can make a difference with our time and talents and resources. By pursuing good financial practices, we free ourselves from debt so that we are able to be in mission to the world. If God calls us to go or to do or to give, we can because we are free.

A key part of experiencing financial and spiritual freedom is found in simplicity and in exercising restraint. I am not suggesting we should never buy anything for ourselves. I am not suggesting we should not buy a new car or go on a vacation or buy new clothes or something else we might want. I am suggesting that, with the help of God, we aim to simplify our lives and silence the voices constantly telling us we need more; that we live counterculturally by actually living below, not above, our means; that we build into our budgets the money to buy with cash instead of credit; and that we build in what we need to be able to live generously and faithfully. And in doing so, we will discover the many gifts of simplicity.

"SIMPLE GIFTS"

The sect of Christians called Shakers were known, among other things, for their simplicity. You may be more familiar with the name as the description of a style of furniture than a religious group. Shaker furniture lacked the flourishes of other styles of furniture made at the time, but it was beautiful and excellently crafted. The Shakers also were known for their songs and for dancing and for joy.

Perhaps the best-known Shaker song is "Simple Gifts," written by Elder Joseph Brackett in 1848. This song, which was sung as the people danced and worshipped, captures the invitation to simplicity:

'Tis the gift to be simple, 'tis the gift to be free,
    'Tis the gift to come down where we ought to be,
And when we find ourselves in the place just right,
    'Twill be in the valley of love and delight.

When true simplicity is gain'd,
    To bow and to bend we shan't be asham'd,
To turn, turn will be our delight,
    Till by turning, turning we come round right.

In the remaining chapters, we will focus on how to simplify our lives, how to better enjoy what we have and give more generously, and how to handle our money and possessions in the way that God intends—and in doing these things, we will find joy.

THINKING IT THROUGH

- There is a balance between making the acquisition of money and possessions your focus and not doing enough to provide for yourself. Read Proverbs 30:7-9. How well do you maintain this balance? What might help you stay in balance?

- Pray and invite God to speak to you through the words of Jesus. Read Matthew 13:1-9, 18-23. What happens to the gospel in our lives when we are consumed with the desire for wealth?

- What does the word covet mean? Read Exodus 20:17 and Ephesians 5:5. How are *covetousness* and *greed* cousins? Why does Paul say that greed is idolatry? In what ways do you experience covetousness? How is greed evidenced in your life?

- Read and reflect on Ecclesiastes 5:10; Matthew 16:26; and 1 Timothy 6:10b. What is God saying to you through these verses?

- Are there signs of affluenza and credit-itis in your life? What most effectively fuels your desire for more?

- What is next on your list of desired items to purchase? Would you say you have more stuff than you have room for, just the right amount, or less stuff than you need?

CHAPTER TWO

WISDOM AND FINANCE

WISDOM AND FINANCE

The plans of the diligent lead surely to abundance,
but everyone who is hasty comes only to want.
Proverbs 21:5

Precious treasure remains in the house of the wise,
but the fool devours it.
Proverbs 21:20

The idea of keeping up with the Joneses is very much alive today. It's a phenomenon that crosses all socioeconomic boundaries and generally results in people living beyond their means. Yet people who live beyond their means are living in a false sense of reality. They're doing a juggling act, often taking cash advances to pay off other lines of credit and making only minimum payments on their credit cards. That is a warning sign of impending financial disaster. Another warning sign is increased consumer debt. If an individual's or family's consumer debt is higher this year than it was last year, then they are heading in the wrong direction.

Perhaps you're not in that place; perhaps you're doing pretty well. For you, the question might not be "Are you heading for a looming financial crisis?" but "Are you making the most of everything that you have, or do you find yourself being wasteful here or there because you can afford to?"

In either case, there is a problem that needs to be addressed. A large part of the problem is that we live in a time of excessive materialism. Many people today are on a treadmill of consumerism, and that treadmill just keeps going faster and faster. But the day will come when either we are going to break down or the treadmill is going to break down, because we cannot continue to go faster and faster in our passion to consume.

In this chapter we will look at biblical wisdom and basic money management principles that can help us manage our money and get back on the right track. Perhaps you are already familiar with these principles in theory but not in practice. So often we're like dieters who know that in order to lose weight they must eat right and exercise, yet still they fail to do so. Similarly, we know many wise money-management principles; yet often we fail to practice them. The purpose of this book is to provide some practical help and encouragement that will help us not only to evaluate our relationship with money and material possessions, but also to become wise stewards of these God-given resources.

THE PRODIGAL IN EACH OF US

Let us begin with one of the primary struggles we face: Many of us have a bit of the prodigal son in us. The prodigal son, who was the younger of two sons, demanded his share of his father's inheritance, left home, and squandered everything. This parable of Jesus, which is found in Luke 15, is a story about the love of God—about how God takes us back even when we've squandered everything we have. Even when we've wandered from the fold, God's mercy is abundant and God joyfully welcomes us home. This is the aspect of the story we typically focus on, but there is another important element of the story.

As the parable begins, Jesus describes the habits of the young man—and they are habits many of us emulate today. Jesus said:

> "There was a man who had two sons. The younger of them said to his father, 'Father, give me the share of the property that will belong to me.' So he divided his property between them. A few days later the younger son gathered all he had and traveled to a distant country, and there he squandered his property in dissolute living.

When he had spent everything, a severe famine took place throughout that country, and he began to be in need. So he went and hired himself out to one of the citizens of that country, who sent him to his fields to feed the pigs. He would gladly have filled himself with the pods that the pigs were eating; and no one gave him anything." (Luke 15:11-16)

From Jesus' description, we see that the prodigal son had the habits of squandering and spending. The word *prodigal* does not mean someone who wanders away or is lost. The word *prodigal* literally means "one who wastes money." A prodigal wastes money and is a spendthrift. Many of us struggle with that habit as well.

The prodigal son wanted his inheritance from his father, and he wanted it *now*. The inheritance was a piece of property that would have been used to supply an income for this young man for the rest of his life. He probably would have grown crops or kept flocks on the property, and that would have provided a livelihood for the rest of his days. But the prodigal son couldn't see it that way. All he wanted was pleasure—instant gratification. He wasn't interested in tomorrow. He was living in the now.

We can relate, can't we? Many of us struggle because we're only thinking about today. We're not thinking about what's going to happen twenty or thirty years from now. Did you know that nearly half of all American workers have less than $25,000 set aside for their retirement?[1] I'm not worried about tomorrow. I want it today. I can have pleasure now. That's what so many of us think, and that's what the younger son thought.

The prodigal son thought his life was about pleasure and wild living. So he took what was his and left his father. I can imagine the father saying, "Please don't do this. If you sell the property, you're going to have nothing. I've saved this for you." But his son wouldn't listen. He was only interested in what he could experience right then. He sold his entire future for what he could have in the moment.

The problem with that kind of thinking is that, for most of us, the famine eventually comes. It comes when we have spent everything we have and even a little bit of next year's income—or perhaps quite a lot of next year's income—and we have nothing left. We've squandered it all. Then the car breaks down, or there are medical needs, or the air conditioning or heating system breaks down, and we find we have no money to pay for those things because we've already leveraged our future. So we use the credit card and charge it, and we go a little further into debt. Finally, we come to a place where we "find ourselves." We have nothing left, not even any credit, and we can't figure out how we are we going to make it. We long for the "pods" that someone else is eating because we simply can't make it on our own anymore.

That is what often happens when we focus on the now and long only to experience pleasure today. When our life purpose is simply enjoying and having as much pleasure as we can in the moment, the things we do tend to become less and less satisfying until, finally, we come to a place where we're entirely dissatisfied—and often broke. This is how many of us live. We waste the opportunities that are before us, selling out for short-term pleasure. We charge our future away.

Others of us do not find ourselves broke. We are not abusing our credit cards. There are no creditors calling and asking for payments. We simply have become wasteful and extravagant, throwing our money away. We burn money on things we neither need nor derive value from—almost recklessly, as if we just need to spend for the sake of spending.

My wife, LaVon, and I are not in financial hardship. We don't abuse our credit cards. We save and we give. We're doing okay. But I've noticed that the more money we make, the more money we waste. It seems that the more financially secure we become, the less we worry about spending money here and there.

When we were starting out together, we struggled to make ends meet. We had to account for every dollar. But today, twenty dollars here and forty dollars there is not a big deal. We waste a dollar on this or that, and we forget where it went. Money just seems to flow through our fingers. And by the end of the year, I'm asking myself, *Where did it all go?* The reason for this is that we're not as careful with our money as we should be. Every dollar we choose to waste is a dollar that could be used for something more meaningful—something that would have lasting impact. It could be saved or invested for retirement or given to help others and support God's kingdom work. When I remember this, I realize that being a good steward of what I have is a matter of great importance.

There are many ways we waste money, but I would like to highlight two of the primary money-wasters that so many of us struggle with. I'm not suggesting that we eliminate these two things altogether; I am suggesting that we simply think more carefully about how we spend our money.

> *"No one can serve two masters; for a slave*
> *will either hate the one and love the other,*
> *or be devoted to the one and despise the*
> *other. You cannot serve God and wealth."*
> *(Matthew 6:24)*

Money-Waster #1: Impulse Buying

The first way we waste money is by impulse buying. When it comes to impulse buying, I am one of the worst offenders. I walk into a store, something catches my attention, and I think,

I've got to have that! Suddenly I must have something that only a few minutes ago I didn't even know I needed. This is especially a problem when I go grocery shopping, which is why I don't go to the grocery store very often!

One day I was going to make chili for supper and realized we needed sour cream (delicious on top of chili!). So I stopped by the grocery store to purchase some. I walked in and saw some beautiful sunflowers in the floral section. I thought, *We've got to have those. They would look so nice on the kitchen table.* So I put them in the basket. Then I walked past the soda aisle and saw that they were having a special. It wasn't the kind of soda I drink, but I thought, *Somebody at our house will drink this if I pick it up.* So I bought three twelve-packs. Then I spotted some chips that looked really good—I suppose I was a little hungry—so I picked them up. I continued down several more aisles finding a variety of things that looked delicious. Finally, I found the sour cream and made my way to check out. In all, I spent over $40 for what should have been a $2 stop at the store—all because I couldn't control myself.

There are two keys to avoiding impulse buys in the grocery store. First, never go grocery shopping when you are hungry! If you do, you are guaranteed to pick up extra items. Second, make a list and stick to it. If you see something else you want, write it down and wait for your next planned shopping trip.

> *"Sell your possessions, and give alms. Make*
> *purses for yourselves that do not wear out,*
> *an unfailing treasure in heaven, where no*
> *thief comes near and no moth destroys.*
> *For where your treasure is, there your heart*
> *will be also." (Luke 12:33-34)*

Another impulse-buying temptation for many of us is sales. One day I was lured into a men's clothing store by a sign in the window with that four-letter word: *SALE*. So I went inside to see what they had. I perused the sale rack and saw a shirt that I liked. Then I noticed that it was half price. Now, I'm somewhat colorblind; but to me the shirt looked nice. I tried it on and quickly decided to buy it. When I took it home, my daughters took one look at it and said, "Dad, that color looks awful on you. You can't wear that!" They asked me what color it was, and I looked at the tag and discovered that the official color name was "latex." Unfortunately, I could not take the shirt back. The sign by the register had been clear: "No returns on sale merchandise." Here's what I did that day: I burned money on a shirt that has hung in my closet ever since. It was an impulse buy.

The rule-of-thumb regarding impulse buys is this: Shop for what you need only. Make a list, buy what you need, and get out of the store! Of course, many of us won't do that; so here's what I have found works for me: I try to wait twenty-four hours before purchasing an impulse buy. I'm amazed at how many things I decide I really don't need after waiting twenty-four hours. Try it for yourself. If you'll just put the brakes on for one day before buying any impulse item, you'll be amazed by how much money you will save.

Money-Waster #2: Eating Out

A second common money-waster is eating out. Now, I'm not suggesting that you should never eat out. The issue is frequency. According to *Kiplinger's Personal Finance* magazine, the average American eats out four times a week.[2] If a family of four were to order burgers with fries and soft drinks at a sit-down restaurant, it would cost—with tax and tip—anywhere from $48 to $55, depending on the restaurant and the area of the country in which they live. And if they were to eat out four times a week, fifty-two weeks a year, they would spend roughly $10,000 or more on eating out in a given year! The cost of preparing the same meal at home—burgers on the grill, homemade fries, soft drinks, and even a healthy vegetable—would be only $15 to $20. The difference is somewhere between 30 and 40 dollars per meal—more than $6,000 per year—money they could save, spend on something more important, or give away.

Again, I'm not suggesting that we never eat out. I'm simply saying that perhaps we eat out too often and the only thing we have to show for it is a spare tire around the waist!

How often do you burn money on eating out? How much money did you spend on eating out last year? And what else might you have done with that money? This leads us to an even bigger and more important question.

WHAT IS YOUR LIFE PURPOSE?

What is your life about? Why do you exist? Do you exist simply to consume as much as you can and get as much pleasure as you can while you are here on this earth, or do you have a higher purpose? How do you understand your life purpose—your vision or mission or calling? And are you spending your money in ways that are consistent with this life purpose? The answers to these questions are very important.

Experience and observation tell me that many of us have not taken the time to think about our life purpose. By default, our society tells us that our life purpose is to consume—to make as much money as possible and to blow as much money as possible. But surely we know that cannot be right.

Remember God's call to Abraham? In the twelfth chapter of Genesis, God essentially says, "Abraham, I've chosen you, and I'm going to bless you. I'm going to make your name great.

And I'm going to increase your descendants so that they will be a great nation. I will bless you so that you might be a blessing to all the nations of the earth" (verses 1-3, author's paraphrase). Like Abraham, we are blessed to be a blessing to others. Our purpose in life is not our own pleasure, as the prodigal son thought. The playwright George Bernard Shaw said it this way in the Epistle Dedicatory in *Man and Superman*:

> This is the true joy in life, the being used for a purpose recognized by yourself as a mighty one; the being thoroughly worn out before you are thrown on the scrap heap; the being a force of Nature instead of a feverish selfish little clod of ailments and grievances complaining that the world will not devote itself to making you happy.[3]

We were created to care for God's creation. We were created to love God and to love our neighbors as ourselves. We were created to care for our families and those in need. We were created to glorify God, to seek justice, and to do mercy. To be a Christian is to follow Jesus Christ and to seek to do his will in our lives. It is to say, "Here I am, all of me! I'm yours. Put me to work, help me serve, use me to accomplish your work."

Now, if this is our life purpose, then our money and possessions should be devoted to helping us fulfill this calling. We are to use our resources to help care for our families and others—to serve Christ and the world through the church, missions, and everyday opportunities. We are blessed to be a blessing.

Barbara Glanz is a motivational speaker who conducts workshops for large companies. One day she was speaking at an event for the employees of a grocery store chain. She talked to them about how they saw their life purpose, suggesting that their work was more than stocking shelves or ringing up customers' food purchases or delivering supplies. She told them that every person they met was an opportunity to bless someone, to live out a higher calling or mission. The employees were inspired by her words, including one nineteen-year-old grocery bagger named Johnny.

Johnny, who has Down syndrome, took her words to heart. He went home and tried to think of ways he could be a blessing to others. Finally, he came up with a plan. Each night he would search the Internet for a positive saying that would encourage people. Then he would print out 300 copies and carefully cut the sayings into individual strips. The next day, he would put one of the sayings in the grocery bag of each of his customers while saying, "I put a saying in your bag. I hope it helps you have a good day. Thanks for coming here."

A month later, the manager noticed that Johnny's line was much longer than the others. Even when he announced that there was no waiting in lines 2 and 3, no one budged. People wanted Johnny to be their bag boy. He touched them and filled them with hope. Johnny got it. He was pursuing a mission that was bigger than his personal satisfaction.[4]

What about each of us? Are we pursuing a mission that is bigger than our personal satisfaction? Can we articulate this mission and its relationship to our faith? Does the allocation of our time and money reflect that mission?

Answering these questions should cause us to reflect on the true role of money and possessions in our lives. Is money, or the things that money can buy, really an appropriate goal or focus for our lives? Is money an end in itself, or is it a means to another end?

Money should never be an end in itself. Rather, it should be a means for accomplishing an end—specifically, for accomplishing our life purpose. Money itself is not bad. It is not the root of all evil. According to the Bible, "the *love* of money is a root of all kinds of evil" (1 Timothy 6:10b, emphasis added). The problem is in how we view or value money. In and of itself, money can be either good or bad depending on how it is used. Money is merely a tool to be used to accomplish the greater purposes God has for our lives.

Part of my own life purpose is to care for my wife and children, and I use a portion of my income to do that. Another part of my life purpose is to further God's kingdom through the local church, and my tithes and offerings help me do that.

I also am called to help the poor and change the world, and I look to my income as an opportunity to do that. In these ways, I use money to accomplish God's purposes in my life.

Each of us is called to be a blessing to others. We have a life purpose that is greater than our own self-interests, and how we spend our God-given resources reflects our understanding and commitment to this life purpose or mission.

SETTING GOALS

Of course, actually being able to accomplish the greater purposes God has for our lives requires some measure of planning. Once we have a sense of our life purpose, the next step is to set some goals. We can begin by asking ourselves, *What do I hope to accomplish in the next year? In the next five years? For the rest of my life?* Then we can set some financial goals that will help us accomplish these objectives—financial goals that are tied to our sense of mission and purpose.

Actually taking the time to set goals related to your life and your finances is crucial if you are to become a wise steward of your God-given resources. Pause right now and think about your life purpose and goals. At the end of this chapter, I have provided a place for you to record two short-term financial goals, two mid-range financial goals, and two long-term financial goals that are aimed at helping you accomplish your broader life goals. At least one goal in each category should relate specifically to your faith.

For example, one of the long-term goals that LaVon and I have set is to give away an increasing percentage of our income each year. One of our short-term goals is to make certain financial commitments toward missions that go above and beyond our tithe that we give to the church. Every year we give our first 10 percent to the church, and then we set aside additional funds from our income. This requires some planning, because otherwise we would simply spend all of our income. In order to increase our giving by one-quarter to one-half of a percent each year, we calculate the amount and set those funds aside in an account so that whenever we see a need or an opportunity, we can freely say, "Hey, we want to help with that."

Setting goals in this way is essential if we are to fulfill a life purpose that moves beyond our own interests to bless the lives of others.

DEVELOPING A PLAN

Once we have set some financial goals, we need to develop a plan to meet those goals. The saying is true: A failure to plan is a plan to fail. Without both goals and a plan to reach those goals, we will revert to being prodigals. A plan gives us concrete steps that we can take to accomplish our goals.

When I was in high school, I wanted to go on a trip to Mexico with my Spanish class. My mom was divorced, and money didn't come easily. I was working at a fast-food restaurant, and I knew that in order to go on the trip, I would have to raise much of the money myself. Mom would help, but she could not pay for all of the expenses. I also had a goal of giving 10 percent of my income away. These were two important goals, and my mom had a simple plan to help me. She took two envelopes and wrote "Mexico Trip" on one and "Tithing" on the other. She told me to fund my envelopes and savings account first, and then I could spend whatever was left. So every week I would cash my paycheck and put 10 percent in my tithing envelope, a percentage into savings, and a chunk into the Mexico trip envelope. Whatever I had left was my spending money for that week. I was able to tithe each week and save enough money for the trip, including some extra spending money, all because my mom helped me devise a plan to accomplish my goals. She taught me the importance of setting goals and funding my goals first, before spending the rest of my money.

When it comes to achieving our financial goals and life purpose, we all need a plan. Some people use an envelope system for saving and spending based on the basic principle of the simple system my mother set up for me in high school. Some set up separate bank accounts for funding various objectives or goals, such as family needs, missions and charitable giving, and retirement savings. Others use a variety of different approaches. Many people find it helpful to seek the advice of a financial advisor, someone who counsels people in how to have good financial practices. For those who find themselves in the midst of a financial crisis, a financial counselor can help work out terms with creditors and develop a workable financial plan. Whatever approach you choose, the important thing is simply to have a plan. (For more suggestions, see a list of 14 Financial Management Tips on pages 146–147.)

There are countless books written by financial experts on the subject of financial planning. My aim here is to be one more voice encouraging you to have healthy financial habits that will enable you to reach your financial goals. After reviewing numerous plans and strategies offered by a variety of financial planners and collaborating with my colleague and partner in ministry Dr. Clayton Smith, I have condensed some of the most basic financial planning concepts into the following six principles:

Six Financial Planning Principles

1. Pay your tithe and offering first.
2. Create a budget and track your expenses.
3. Simplify your lifestyle (live below your means).
4. Establish an emergency fund.

5. Pay off your credit cards, use cash/debit cards for purchases, and use credit wisely.
6. Practice long-term savings and investing habits.

Let's briefly review each of these principles.

First, pay your tithe and offering first. In other words, put God first in your living and your giving. Make it your number one priority to honor God with what you have. Give your tithe and offering from the "top" of your paycheck, and then live on whatever remains.

Second, create a budget and track your expenses. Creating a budget is simply developing a plan in which you tell your money what you want it to do. Tracking your expenses with a budget is like getting on the scales: It allows you to see how you are doing and motivates you to be more careful with your expenditures.

Third, simplify your lifestyle. Simplifying your lifestyle is essentially learning to live below your means. Because this discipline is critical to the success of your financial plan, I have devoted the following section and the entire next chapter to this topic.

Fourth, establish an emergency fund. An emergency fund is an account separate from checking or long-term savings that is set aside specifically for emergencies—hence the name. Then, when an emergency arises—such as an unexpected car repair, medical need, or home repair—you will not have to pull out a credit card but can tap into your emergency fund. Dave Ramsey recommends beginning with $1,000 and building that to three months' worth of income.[5] When you have this amount, you won't need to use your credit cards anymore.

Fifth, pay off your credit cards, use cash/debit cards for purchases, and use credit wisely. As you are building your emergency fund, begin to pay off your credit card debt and start using cash or debit cards for purchases. Whenever you need or want something, use only the money you have on hand or in the bank. If an item costs more money than you have available, save up for the purchase. Ramsey and a host of others recommend paying off the cards as quickly as possible. Some suggest starting with the credit card that has the highest interest rate. Others, like Ramsey, suggest you pay down the smallest debt first, experience that victory, and begin applying your payments from the first card to the second, and so on, creating a snowball effect to pay off the cards as soon as possible. They speak of the importance of freeing yourself from credit cards by having what they call "plastic surgery"—cutting up your cards as you pay them down so that your future is not leveraged for present-day pleasure, as the prodigal son's was.

Some financial advisors acknowledge that once you have paid off your credit card debt, there may be times when you need to use a credit card, such as when traveling or making purchases online. They urge, however, that you pay off the debt monthly. If you are unable to do this, then it really is better for you to cut up your cards and stop using them altogether. (See more techniques for paying off credit cards on page 148.)

Sixth, practice long-term savings and investing habits. Saving money is the number one wise money management principle everyone should practice. We do not save merely for the sake of saving. There is a word for that: hoarding. Hoarding is frowned upon in the Bible as the practice of fools and those who fail to understand the purpose of life. Saving, on the other hand, is meant to be purposeful.

There are three types of savings we should have: (1) emergency savings, which we have already discussed; (2) savings for wants and goals; and (3) retirement savings. The first two categories keep us from being a slave to the credit card company. Saving for wants and goals is setting aside money in advance for things we know we will need or want, rather than buying them on credit. This includes things such as televisions, cars, and even college. For larger savings goals and needs, consider routinely deducting a percentage from your paycheck and depositing this amount in a savings account or investment option. Set up a direct deposit so that the money is automatically deducted from your paycheck and deposited into the appropriate account. Do not have a debit card on your savings account, and do not link your savings account to your checking account so that it is easy to transfer money from your savings to your checking.

The third type of savings is for retirement. People are living longer today than ever before. You likely will live into your nineties and may even pass one hundred. This is one of many reasons that Social Security will be in crisis in the future. It is really important that we make it a priority to set aside some funds for our retirement, particularly when we are young so that time and interest work to our benefit.

Here is one retirement savings plan that begins at age eighteen. Set aside $25 per month for retirement, increasing that amount each year by $25 per month while in college. Upon graduation, add an additional $100 per month to this fund, to bring the total to $200 per month. If you do not go to college and begin working full-time out of high school, or if you are already in the workforce now, start saving $200 per month if possible.

If you were to begin this plan at age eighteen, work your way up to $200 per month, and continue saving this amount monthly until retirement, carefully investing the money in a Roth Individual Retirement Account, you would have over one million dollars at retirement. Add that to whatever small amount you might receive from Social Security and any other retirement benefit, such as an employer's pension plan, and you will be able to take care of your needs, continue to live generously, and enjoy life in the "golden years." But heed this word of warning: Every year you wait to start, you are missing out on another year of accumulated interest. A financial counselor is always a good resource to consult when making decisions regarding retirement and other long-term savings needs.

So, these six principles combined create a simple plan to help you become a better money manager. I invite you to try this plan, as well as to seek out additional help and resources for creating a more in-depth, comprehensive financial plan tailored to your specific goals and objectives. Remember, the prodigal son was welcomed home and loved by his father; but he had to make a new start. So do we!

SIMPLIFYING YOUR LIFESTYLE

Making a new start so that we may achieve financial peace and accomplish God's greater purposes for our lives requires us to do one of two things: Either we must make more money, or we must spend less money in order to have money for the things that are most important to us. These are our only two options. Most of us cannot control whether or not we are going to make more money; increasing our income simply may not be a possibility. But we all can choose to spend less and simplify our lives. We can decide that there are some financial habits we've been practicing that we will forgo for the sake of doing God's will.

If you want to be able to give money when a great cause arises or go on a mission trip or achieve some other financial goal you have set, most likely you will need to simplify your life in order to have the money you need. Perhaps choosing to take your lunch to work more often or going to fewer movies or bargain shopping could help you fund that mission trip or provide a nest egg for your retirement. We give up something in order to have something else. We keep track of our funds and make a conscious effort not to burn or waste any money that could go to something more important. We simplify.

> *Honor the LORD with your substance*
> *and with the first fruits of all your*
> *produce. (Proverbs 3:9)*

Perhaps you are trapped by a house payment for a home you cannot afford or maintain. Could God be calling you to simplify—to trade down and discover hundreds if not thousands of dollars you can now use for doing the things that matter to you? Perhaps you need to eat out one less meal a week, using the money you save to go on a mission trip or buy meals for those who are homeless. Think about it: Which would you still be talking about five years from now—encouraging and caring for the poor, or eating out one extra meal a week?

> *Do not wear yourself out to get rich; be*
> *wise enough to desist. When your eyes light*
> *upon it, it is gone; for suddenly it takes*
> *wings to itself, flying like an eagle toward*
> *heaven. (Proverbs 23:4-5)*

Years ago, I was having lunch with a church member. He was the vice president of his company—well respected and quite successful. He lived in a large house—nice, but not too extravagant. He drove nice cars. On that particular day at lunch he was excited. He said, "I bought a new car this week." I said, "Really? What did you buy?" He said, "I'll show you after lunch."

We went out to the parking lot after lunch, and I expected to see a new BMW. To my surprise he pointed to a seven-year-old Honda Civic. I said, "Tell me about this car." He said, "It is a cream puff, one-owner, low-miles, always garaged car. I paid cash for it, and the insurance and the taxes were nothing. It is fun to drive."

I said, "You surprise me. What's up here?" And he said, "I just realized that I could do other things with the money I was spending on a car—things that were more important to me. Since my life mission and purpose is taking a new turn, I felt like I could use that money to support that." As he drove off that day, do you think I admired him less or more?

Which do you find more admirable in a person—someone who is living at the edge of his or her means and thus cannot do the things that really matter, or someone who lives below his or her means and has a meaningful life of purpose? Do you admire the one who lives extravagantly, or the one who gives extravagantly?

In order to give extravagantly and experience the joy that comes from living for something beyond ourselves, we must simplify our lives. Remember the words of the Shaker song "Simple Gifts,"

'Tis the gift to be simple, 'tis the gift to be free . . .

THINKING IT THROUGH

- How would you define or describe your life purpose?

- What are three goals that can help you achieve this life purpose?

- What are some financial goals that can help support your life goals and purpose?

Short-term financial goals (next 12 months):

1.

2.

Mid-range financial goals (2 to 5 years):

1.

2.

Long-term financial goals (5 years to retirement):

1.

2.

BUDGET WORKSHEET

Item	Actual %	Suggested %*	Plan for next 12 months
Housing		25–35%	
Transportation		10–15%	
Charitable Gifts		10–12%	
Food		5–15%	
Savings		5–10%	
Utilities		5–10%	
Medical/Health		5–10%	
Debt		5–10%	
Clothing		2–7%	
Miscellaneous		12–23%	

*These percentages are adapted from Dave Ramsey's *The Total Money Makeover* (Nashville: Thomas Nelson, 2007).

CHAPTER THREE

CULTIVATING CONTENTMENT

CULTIVATING CONTENTMENT

*And [Jesus] said to them, "Take care! Be on your
guard against all kinds of greed; for one's life does
not consist in the abundance of possessions."*
Luke 12:15

*Whatever my eyes desired I did not keep from them; I kept
my heart from no pleasure. . . . Then I considered all that my
hands had done and the toil I had spent in doing it,
and again, all was vanity and a chasing after wind.*
Ecclesiastes 2:10-11

I n 2017, large areas of California were ravaged by wildfires. Dozens of people were killed, and tens of thousands were evacuated from their homes. As I watched the tragedy unfold via television news coverage, it struck me that this was a moment in which so many people were being forced to think about their relationship to material possessions. The words of Jesus echoed in my ears every time I saw another picture of the raging fires: "One's life does not consist in the abundance of possessions" (Luke 12:15).

So many people had very little notice that the fires were coming their direction. Thousands had just minutes to grab everything they could take from their homes and flee.

After a similarly devastating outbreak of wildfires a decade earlier, *Time* magazine's online edition asked people who had been moved to emergency shelters: "What did you save from the fire?"[1]

Andrew saved his pillow.

Shervi saved her family pictures and books.

Angel saved the saxophone he had been learning to play.

Karen saved her two cats and important documents.

Michelle saved her Bible, purse, shoes, diploma, and cell phone.

What would you save? Imagine a wildfire is headed toward your home and you have ten minutes to grab what you can and flee. What will you take with you?

Natural disasters remind us that everything in this world is temporary. If our stuff is taken away by bankruptcy or plundered by thieves or blown away by a tornado or burned in a wildfire, we must remember that material things are only temporary. When I'm gone, most of my stuff will be outdated, worn out, or simply of no value to anyone else—either hawked in a garage sale or thrown in the trash. This is why I can say with Jesus, "[My] life does not consist in the abundance of possessions."

I believe that. I believe it, first, because Jesus said it. I also believe it because somehow I intuitively know that it's true. But there is a problem: Everywhere I turn, the world is telling me that it's not true. The world continually tells me that my life *does* consist in the abundance of my possessions. I am bombarded with messages such as, *If you had a little bit more, you'd be happier. If you had this thing that you currently do not have, you'd find more satisfaction in life. If you had a bigger house or a nicer car or more fashionable clothes, you'd be happy—at least happier than you are right now.*

Each of us is bombarded with messages such as these daily. While Jesus is telling us that our lives consist of more than money or things, the culture is shouting that it's not true. The result is a wrestling in our hearts. Despite the fact that we say we believe Jesus' words, we still find ourselves devoting a great deal of our time, talents, and resources to the acquisition of more stuff. We say that our lives do not consist in the abundance of our possessions, but we live as if they do.

As we saw in the preceding chapter, most of us are afflicted with affluenza and credit-itis. I believe we also are afflicted with another dangerous condition: Restless Heart Syndrome.

RESTLESS HEART SYNDROME (RHS)

Perhaps you've heard of restless legs syndrome (RLS), a condition in which one has twitches and contractions in the legs. A condition I call Restless Heart Syndrome (RHS) works in a similar way, but in the heart—or soul. Its primary symptom is discontent. We find that we are never satisfied with anything. The moment we acquire something, we scarcely take time to enjoy it before we want something else. We are perennially discontent. This is the nature of RHS, and it is a syndrome that, if left unchecked, can destroy us.

Now, there is a certain discontent that God intended us to have. God actually wired our hearts so that they would be discontent with certain things, causing us to seek the only One who can fully satisfy us. God wants us to be content with certain things and discontent with others. The problem is that we tend to get them confused. We tend to be discontent with those things we are supposed to be content with, and content with those things we are supposed to be discontent with!

James Mackintosh, the great Scottish philosopher and politician of the late eighteenth and early nineteenth centuries, said this: "It is right to be contented with what we have, but never with what we are."[2] In other words, it is a positive motivator to be discontent with our moral character, our spiritual life, our pursuit of holiness, our desire for justice, and our ability to love. These are areas in which we should continue to grow and improve, for we are meant to become more than we are today. We are meant to yearn to know God more, to cultivate a deeper prayer life, to pursue justice and holiness with increasing fervor, to love others more, and to grow in grace and character and wisdom with each passing day. The problem is that we tend to be content with our involvement in pursuing justice in the world. We tend to be content with our level of righteousness—sometimes being self-righteous. We tend to be content with how much we love others. We tend to be content with our relationship with God. We tend to be content with how often we read the Bible and pray. Generally, we are satisfied with those things that deserve more of our time and attention.

Likewise, those things we should be content with are the very things we find ourselves hopelessly discontented with. Most of us, for example, experience discontentment with our stuff—our homes, cars, televisions, gadgets, clothes, and a whole host of other things. We buy our dream home, and two weeks later we notice that the kitchen isn't quite right and the appliances really don't meet our needs and the builder's-grade carpet isn't quite nice enough. So, the moment we move in, we begin thinking about the improvements we'd like to make. We're just not completely happy with the house of our dreams. Then there's the car we couldn't wait to buy. We think it is great until we drive it off the lot. Before the new-car smell has dissipated, we are already thinking about the next car we want to get. We seem to look for reasons to be unhappy with our stuff so that we can go out and buy new stuff.

> *Keep your lives free from the love of money,*
> *and be content with what you have; for he*
> *has said, "I will never leave you or forsake*
> *you." So we can say with confidence,*
> *"The Lord is my helper; I will not be*
> *afraid." (Hebrews 13:5-6)*

At one time or another, most of us also find ourselves discontented with our jobs. In fact, many of us are constantly searching for a new job. Even while at work, we're looking online to see if there's a better job out there somewhere. Perhaps we don't like our boss, so we decide the answer is to find something else. Maybe it's not the boss; maybe it's the work environment or the pay. Nevertheless, we're continually searching for the perfect job that will make us happy.

Many of us do the same thing when it comes to the church. We have an illusion that things are going to be perfect in the church. So when we begin to see all of the "warts," we become discontented. There's that usher who wasn't very friendly to us, and that time the pastor said something that hurt our feelings, and the incident when no one called after we volunteered for something; and before long, all we can see is what's wrong with the church. We can't see the good stuff anymore. So we go church shopping and find another church. We hang around there for a couple of years until our feelings get hurt or we are disappointed in some way, and then we go looking for another church again. Somehow we believe the grass is always greener on the other side.

We did this with our parents when we were teenagers. We thought, *Man, I wish Mike's mom and dad were my parents. If I had his parents, I wouldn't have all these problems. I'd be really happy. His parents let him stay out until 12:30 a.m. My parents make me come in at midnight.* What we didn't know was that Mike was thinking, *I wish I had her parents. If her parents were my parents, I'd be really happy. They're so nice. Mine are so mean.*

Of course, we do the very same thing as parents. We say to our kids, "How come so-and-so's children are so respectful and you're not?" Our kids bring their friends over to spend the night, and we joke, "Would you like to come and live with us?" The problem is that if they stayed, they'd become monsters in our house, too. That's how it works.

The same kind of thing happens in our marriages. We're madly in love when we get married. All we can see are the wonderful attributes of our mate. But after a while, we begin to see only those things that irritate us, frustrate us, and drive us crazy. Then one day we notice someone else and think, *If only I had met this person sooner!* or *If only my wife/husband was like so-and-so.* Suddenly we find ourselves comparing our mate to others, focusing on his or her imperfections and imagining how much happier we would be if we were married to someone else. But just as it is with stuff and jobs and churches and parents and children, so it is with spouses: There are no perfect ones. The person we think would make us happy has his or her own idiosyncrasies that would drive us crazy after a while.

This is what our discontent does to us. Sometimes I think God must look down on us and feel the way we feel when we give someone we really care for a special gift and he or she asks for the gift receipt. God must look at us and think, *What is it with these people? I give them all of this, and they keep asking for the gift receipt.* It's as if we're saying to God, "I don't like what you have given me, God, and I want something else. I want to trade it in and get something better than what you gave me."

Clearly, we have RHS. We struggle with discontentment. So, what can we do about it? I would like to suggest four ways we can cultivate contentment in the appropriate areas of our lives, followed by five ways to simplify our lives. I have found that the two go hand in hand. When we simplify, we are content; and when we are content, we simplify.

FOUR WAYS TO CULTIVATE CONTENTMENT

The apostle Paul is an excellent example of contentment. He wrote, "I have learned to be content with whatever I have.

I know what it is to have little, and I know what it is to have plenty. In any and all circumstances I have learned the secret of being well-fed and of going hungry, of having plenty and of being in need" (Philippians 4:11-12). When Paul wrote these words, he was sitting in a prison cell in Rome, waiting for the news of whether or not he would be executed. On a trip to Rome, I actually visited this prison cell and discovered that Paul was lowered through a hole in the floor and dropped into a cavernous, damp pit. This is where he sat when he wrote these words in his Letter to the Philippians, which is known as his letter of joy.

Like Paul, we too can learn to be content in whatever circumstances we may find ourselves. These four keys, which include the "secret" Paul referred to in his letter, can help us do that.

> *I have learned to be content with whatever*
> *I have. I know what it is to have little,*
> *and I know what it is to have plenty.*
> *In any and all circumstances I have learned*
> *the secret of being well-fed and of going*
> *hungry, of having plenty and of being*
> *in need. (Philippians 4:11-12)*

1. Remember that it could be worse.

This first key to contentment comes from John Ortberg, pastor at Menlo Park Presbyterian Church in California. He says there are four words we should say whenever we find ourselves discontented with something or someone: *It could be worse.*

Ortberg suggests that when you are getting into your five-year-old car in the parking lot, say, "It could be worse." As you walk into your apartment or condo or house that is in desperate need of repairs, say, "It could be worse." When you go to work and are faced with problems and difficulties and disappointments, say, "It could be worse." And when you're frustrated and disappointed with your spouse, say, "It could be worse." Actually, Ortberg suggests you *think* the words this time, rather than say them aloud!

This is essentially the practice of looking on the bright side or finding the silver lining. It is recognizing that no matter what we may not like about a thing or person or circumstance, we can always find something good to focus on if only we will choose to do so.

2. Ask yourself, "How long will this make me happy?"

The second key to contentment is asking yourself a simple question: How long will this make me happy? So often we buy something, thinking it will make us happy, only to find that the happiness lasts about as long as it takes to open the box. There is a moment of satisfaction when we make the purchase, but the item does not continue to bring satisfaction over a period of time. Many of the things we buy are simply not worth the expense.

Have you ever thought you simply had to have something and later found out that it wasn't that much fun after all? Several years ago when I was visiting my brother, I watched him playing a game on his PlayStation 2 (PS2). Later I told my wife, LaVon, that I really wanted to get one. She said, "Who are you kidding? You're not going to play with it. You don't have time for that." I assured her that I would. So I saved up, went to the mall, and bought a PS2, along with four video games. That was several years ago, and to this day I have played only half of one game. One day the whole kit and caboodle will be in a rummage sale for ten or fifteen bucks.

I have learned that it is a good idea to try before you buy. A few years ago, I thought I needed a particular kind of car. So I decided I would rent one before buying it. The next time I was scheduled to speak in another city, I rented this kind of car for two days for $49.99 a day. After driving the car two days I found I no longer felt the desire for a new car. I dropped the car off at the rental car location content to continue to drive my old car for a few more years. That $100 I spent saved me $20,000!

Rent the car of your dreams for a weekend—or that vacation home—or borrow someone else's new gadget and see what you think. Then decide if you still want to buy. It's amazing how often we change our minds when we try before we buy and stop to ask ourselves, "How long will this make me happy?"

3. Develop a grateful heart.

The third key to contentment is to develop a grateful heart. This is one of the most important keys to contentment and happiness in life. Gratitude is essential if we are to be content.

The apostle Paul said that we are to "give thanks in all circumstances" (1 Thessalonians 5:18). A grateful heart recognizes that all of life is a gift. Contentment comes when we spend more time giving thanks for what we have than thinking about what's missing or wrong in our lives. In any situation, we either can complain or be grateful. We can focus on all the things we don't like, or we can begin to search for the things we do like and be grateful for them. We can focus on the disappointments, or we can give thanks for the blessings.

> *Give thanks in all circumstances; for this is*
> *the will of God in Christ Jesus for you.*
> *(1 Thessalonians 5:18)*

A man once told me that one night he and his wife had an argument. He was so angry that he walked out the door and headed down the street. He walked for about half a mile before he calmed down. Then he began to pray as he walked, listing all the things his wife did that frustrated and irritated him. After a while his prayer took a different turn, and he began to thank God for the traits in his wife that had led to his frustration. "Thank you that she is strong-willed, that she has a fiery personality, and that she calls me to be better than I am," he prayed. Before long, he was thanking God for the things that he had always loved about her: "Thank you for her touch, her smile, her eyes, her kiss, her embrace, her beauty." By the time he walked back into the house, his heart had changed from anger to gratitude. He felt truly grateful for the precious gift God had given him in his wife.

Sometimes feelings of love come after we talk about love and express love. We say, "I love you," and do loving things, and eventually we have loving feelings. We think the feelings should come first, but it works the other way around. Likewise, when we begin to be grateful and express gratitude to God, over time we find our hearts have changed and we are grateful for what we have. Then we are able to be content.

4. Ask yourself, "Where does my soul find true satisfaction?"

The fourth key to contentment is found in this question: *Where does my soul find true satisfaction?* The world answers this question by telling us that we find satisfaction in ease and luxury and comfort and money. The Bible, however, answers the question very differently. From Genesis to Revelation, it tells us that we find our satisfaction in God alone.

As we've discussed previously, our restless hearts are meant to seek after God. This is why Saint Augustine's words, written more than 1,600 years ago, still ring true today: "Thou hast made us for thyself, O Lord, and our hearts are restless until they find their rest in thee." The psalmist said it this way: "O God, you are my God, I seek you, / my soul thirsts for you. . . . / My soul is satisfied as with a rich feast, / and my mouth praises you with joyful lips / when I think of you on my bed, / and meditate on you in the watches of the night" (63:1, 5-6).

The apostle Paul named the source of his soul's satisfaction in his Letter to the Philippians when he wrote, "I can do all things *through [Christ]* who strengthens me" (4:13, emphasis added). In other words, he found Christ to be his Source, the One who satisfied his every need and enabled him to be content in all circumstances—whether in a prison cell or a palace, whether in poverty or in wealth. This was Paul's "secret" to contentment (verse 12). Paul had discovered the deep love of God. He knew that his life belonged to God and that he was a part of God's plans for the world. All of his deepest needs were satisfied in his relationship with God through Christ.

Deep in our hearts we, too, desire to be connected with the One who is the Creator of the universe. We need to believe our lives have meaning. We need to know there is grace and mercy when we have blown it. We need to know there is hope in the face of the darkest circumstances. We need to know we are loved unconditionally by Someone who knows us better than we know ourselves. And we need to be able to share this love in meaningful relationships with others. Contentment is found in our relationship with God and our relationships with others. This is why Jesus said the two most important things we must do are to "love the Lord your God with all your heart, and with all your soul, and with all your mind" and to "love your neighbor as yourself" (Matthew 22:37, 39). If we keep our focus on these two things, we will find satisfaction for our souls and lasting contentment.

Contrary to what the world would have us believe, the longings of our souls cannot be satisfied at the shopping mall. The writer of the Book of Ecclesiastes, presumably Solomon in his later years, considered everything life has to offer and said that all is vanity, a chasing after the wind. He wrote, "Whatever my eyes desired I did not keep from them; I kept my heart from no pleasure. . . . Then I considered all that my hands had done and the toil I had spent in doing it, and again, all was vanity and a chasing after wind" (2:10-11).

The only real satisfaction of our souls is Jesus Christ. We can be content because we know Christ is by our side no matter what we're walking through. The writer of the

Book of Hebrews said it this way: "Keep your lives free from the love of money, and be content with what you have; for [Christ] has said, 'I will never leave you or forsake you.' So we can say with confidence, 'The Lord is my helper; I will not be afraid'" (13:5-6). With this assurance, we can face whatever each day may bring with contentment and joy.

FIVE WAYS TO SIMPLIFY OUR LIVES

In addition to cultivating contentment in our lives, we also need to cultivate simplicity. As mentioned, contentment and simplicity go hand in hand.

Simplicity says less is more. Simplicity says we do not need as much clutter in our lives. In fact, the more we pursue "more," the more stressed out we become. After all, more stuff means more maintenance, which involves time, energy, and resources. The truth is that more stuff makes us less happy. There comes a point when we have enough stuff, and everything above and beyond that level only creates stress.

When I think of the stress created by our relentless pursuit of stuff, I think of a hamster running on a wheel. The hamster gets on the wheel, not knowing where it is going. It starts running faster and faster until one of two things happens:

Either it flies off the wheel into the side of the cage, exhausted, or the hamster wheel breaks.

That is the image that comes to mind when I look at current consumerism trends. We are like a hamster on a wheel. We really don't know where we are going, but we are sure everybody else does; so we run faster and faster to keep up. Eventually, something is sure to break—the system or us or both. Many would say this is what is happening right now in our nation.

Without question, our consuming habits have serious consequences that affect not only our personal and national debt, but also our world. Consider, for example, our consumption of renewable and non-renewable resources. Every year Americans consume over 1.2 billion trees to support our needs for packaging, paper, napkins, and bags. We use 2.5 million plastic bottles every hour—most of these for water. We represent only 5 percent of the world's population, yet we produce 40 percent of the world's garbage—an average of 1,609 pounds per person per year.[3] This is not only wasteful; it is unsustainable. If the rate of our consumption continues to increase each year, as it has for some time, it soon will outpace the growth of the population. We cannot continue this trend and think that everything will be okay. Eventually, we will exceed the rate at which resources can be renewed.

We simply cannot keep going faster and faster, consuming more and more, without devastating consequences—

personally, nationally, and globally. As people of faith who know the true source of our satisfaction, we must agree that sometimes less is more. We must be willing to simplify. We must make a conscious decision to step off the hamster wheel.

Many people are, in fact, embracing the idea of voluntary simplicity, choosing to take a step down in their lifestyle rather than constantly push upward. There are countless ways to do this. I'd like to offer five ideas that I have tried personally and found to be effective.

1. Set a goal of reducing your consumption and choose to live below your means.

Set a tangible goal to reduce your own personal consumption and the production of waste in your life. For example, you might set a goal to reduce your trash consumption by just 10 percent. A simple way to do this is to use canvas bags when you go grocery shopping and to refuse any extra packaging. Another habit I've adopted is to grab only one or two napkins, as opposed to a handful, whenever I eat at a fast-food restaurant. If we all did this, who knows how many napkins we might save!

Whenever you are making purchases, look at the mid-grade instead of the top-of-the-line product. Think slightly smaller than you had planned.

If you are buying a new car, why not aim to improve fuel economy over your existing car by at least 10 percent? If your current car gets 16 miles to the gallon, look for a car that gets 17.6 miles per gallon or better.

Make it your goal to reduce your utilities usage by 10 percent. Set the thermostat back a couple of degrees when you are away during the day and asleep at night, and throw an extra blanket on the bed. Instead of 69 degrees, for example, set it back to 67 degrees. There are even thermostats you can purchase that allow you to program the thermostat so that the adjustments are made automatically.

There are countless other ways to reduce your consumption and live below your means. Do some research, share ideas with others, or have a brainstorming session with your family.

2. Before making a purchase, ask yourself, "Do I really need this?" and "Why do I want this?"

These questions will help you determine the true motivation of your desired purchase. Is it a need, a self-esteem issue, or something else? You may find yourself wrestling with your true motive and decide that your reason for purchasing the item is not a good one.

A high school student told me that if they don't have what he wants when he goes to the electronics store, he feels obligated to walk up and down the aisles until he finds something to buy. Many of us can relate. As I suggested in the previous chapter, use the twenty-four-hour rule. When you see something you think you must have, wait twenty-four hours before making the purchase. If you still feel you should buy the item after waiting a full day, go back and get it. Likewise, remember to try before you buy. These habits will give you time to examine your real motives and make wiser purchasing decisions.

3. Use something up before buying something new.

Though I realize it is not always possible to do this, generally it is. From household items to appliances to cars—wait until a replacement is truly necessary. Take good care of the things you buy and use them until they are empty, broken, or worn out. Buy things that are made to last, and, when buying things that have a short life span, spend your money wisely.

Take better care of your furniture, appliances, and other things around the house. Resole your shoes. Mend rips and tears and make repairs. Remind yourself that you don't always need to have new things. If you feel something is really outdated, keep it for an extra six months or year before replacing it. And finally, always sell or donate things that still work. Who knows how many televisions and toaster ovens and refrigerators that still work have been taken to the dump. Somebody could have used them.

4. Plan low-cost entertainment that enriches.

When it comes to choosing entertainment for your family or friends, plan things that are simple and cheap. You'll be amazed at how much more pleasure you derive from low-cost, simple activities.

Sometimes we go on vacation and spend a ton of money, running here and there and doing this and that, and we're exhausted by the time we get back home. We need a vacation to rest up from the vacation we just took! All we really needed was to lie around and read and play cards and relax. When I look back over the last twenty years and all the things we have done with our kids, I realize that simple activities such as playing games around a table were the most enriching times.

Personally, my favorite activity is to invite friends over to my house. Everyone brings something, we light a fire in the fireplace if the weather is cool, and we sit around and play cards. Usually the simple things are the most fun. For some reason, we think we have to spend money to have fun. That's just not so. Simplify your entertainment choices.

5. Ask yourself, "Are there major changes that would allow me to simplify my life?"

Some of us are living beyond our means, and the stress is killing us. We have in our minds that we can't possibly sell the house or the car. Yes, we can! I can't tell you how much stress relief and joy can be found in selling a car and buying one you pay for in full. It's freeing not to be anxious every month about how you're going to pay the car note. If your car is already paid off, consider keeping it for another year or two before buying another one.

Likewise, you might consider downsizing your home. Houses in America just keep getting bigger and bigger, yet with bigger houses come higher utility costs, more square feet to clean, higher property taxes and insurance, and more furniture to buy.

Is there a club membership you hardly ever use? Perhaps that money might be spent on something more meaningful, such as mission work, a ministry opportunity, or helping someone in your community. Asking yourself questions related to your home, possessions, job, and activities can help you identify some significant changes that will simplify your life.

Remember, if you cannot do all the things God is calling you to do and you're unable to find joy in your life, perhaps it's time to simplify in some major ways.

THE POWER OF SELF-CONTROL

Simplifying your life requires the practice of self-control. Solomon wrote, "Like a city whose walls are broken through / is a person who lacks self-control" (Proverbs 25:28 NIV). When a city's walls are broken through, the enemy can march right in and destroy it. There is no longer any protection. Likewise, self-control is a wall around your heart and life that protects you from yourself, from temptation, and from sins that are deadly and that ultimately can destroy you.

The person who does not exercise self-control in the area of speech constantly says things that hurt others and in the end has no friends. The person with no self-control in the area of eating is constantly overeating and ultimately struggles with health problems. The person who does not exercise self-control when it comes to material possessions leads his or her family to financial ruin because he or she is unable to be satisfied. The opposite of self-control is slavery.

> *Like a city whose walls are broken through*
> *is a person who lacks self-control.*
> *(Proverbs 25:28)*

Self-control comes down to making a choice between satisfying an impulse to gain instant gratification and choosing not to act upon the opportunity for instant gratification for some higher cause or greater gratification later. Often we act impulsively without even thinking.

Self-control is about forgoing instant gratification by stopping to think about the answers to three questions:

- What are the long-term consequences of this action?
- Is there a higher good or a better outcome if I use this resource of time, money, or energy in another way?

• Will this action honor God?

When we stop to ask these three questions, we begin to move beyond being enslaved by our impulses toward exercising self-control. Once we ask these questions, we often find strength and help for pursuing the right course by talking with others, enlisting their support, and praying for God's help and strength in exercising self-control. Then we begin to discover the incredible power of self-control—power that enables us to simplify our lives and experience true contentment.

WHICH "TENT" WILL YOU LIVE IN?

Which "tent" will you live in—discon-tent-ment or con-tent-ment?[4] You and you alone determine which "tent" will be yours. You choose it in large part by deciding what life is about. If you decide that "life does not consist in the abundance of your possessions," then you are choosing contentment.

Choosing contentment does not mean that we must stop buying things or move into cramped homes or apartments. That is not realistic, and I do not believe that is what God requires of us. Rather, choosing contentment means we look to God as our Source, giving thanks for what we have. It means we ask God to give us the right perspective on money and possessions and to change our hearts each day. It means we decide to live simpler lives, wasting less and conserving more. And it means we give more generously, a topic we will examine in the next chapter. When we do these things, we are reclaiming the joy of contentment and simplicity.

> *"Contentment makes poor men rich, but discontentment makes rich men poor."*
> —*Benjamin Franklin*

I have a black suit that is a symbol of contentment and simplicity for me. Every pastor needs at least one nice black suit, and I bought mine sixteen years ago. It was the nicest suit I had ever purchased at the time, bought for half-price at the end of the season at a local department store. I wore it for the first time to a worship service when our church was meeting in an elementary school. I decided then that it was a bit too dressy and that I would save it for weddings, funerals, and special services. Since then, I've worn it to every candlelight Christmas Eve service, every Easter service, every new building dedication service, and almost every wedding and funeral I've conducted. Every so often I think it's time to replace it. No doubt it is slightly out of style. But then I tell myself it is still in good shape, and I think of all the memories I have of times when I've worn it. I've actually told my wife that I want to be buried in that double-breasted black suit.

That suit represents how I hope to live in every area of my consuming—buying things that last, using them up before discarding them, recognizing the value in things that have been around for a while, and pursuing simplicity as a means to contentment. These are among the keys to finding true joy.

THINKING IT THROUGH

- According to Hebrews 13:5-6, what is both our motivation and empowerment for being content with what we have? What effect does contentment have on our outlook and attitude?

- Read Luke 12:15. How are these words of Jesus contrary to the message of the world? What steps can you take to "be on guard" against materialism and greed in your everyday life?

- Read Ecclesiastes 2:10-11. What things and pleasures to which you devote your time, energy, and money are "vanity and a chasing after wind"? Pray, asking God to reveal any changes you need to make in these areas.

- Review the four ways to cultivate contentment. Which one is most challenging for you?

- Make a list of all the things you are grateful for, and offer your thanks to God. Keep this list handy and refer to it often. Add additional blessings as you think of them.

- What are some practical ways you can reduce your personal consumption and the production of waste in your life? What are three tangible goals you can set?

- Are there major changes you can make related to your activities, job, home, car, or other possessions that would allow you to simplify your life? What is one significant change you will strive to make in the coming year?

- What do you and your family enjoy doing for entertainment? How much money do you generally spend on these activities? What are some simple, low-cost entertainment ideas you might try instead? Choose one and make plans to try it in the next week or two.

CHAPTER FOUR

DEFINED BY GENEROSITY

CHAPTER FOUR

DEFINED BY GENEROSITY

*As for those who ... are rich, command them
not to be haughty, or to set their hopes on the
uncertainty of riches, but rather on God who richly
provides us with everything for our enjoyment.*
1 Timothy 6:17

*Some give freely, yet grow all the richer;
others withhold what is due, and only suffer want.
A generous person will be enriched,
and one who gives water will get water.*
Proverbs 11:24-25

When I meet with families to plan a funeral or memorial
service for a loved one, I always ask, "Tell me about
your loved one. What were his/her defining characteristics?"
Even if I knew the individual well, there usually is much I did

not know. As the family members begin to name characteristics, I write them down in a notebook. Then I ask, "What would your loved one have wanted to be remembered for?" Likewise, I write those things down. Later, as I am developing the message for the service, I am able to refer back to my notes and make mention of those defining characteristics.

Someday, someone will sit with our family or friends and ask those same questions. What will the answers be? It can be helpful to pause and think about what we hope people will say were our defining characteristics. Of course, thinking about this too often would be morbid and narcissistic! But now and then, considering how we want others to remember us can be a constructive exercise.

One of the defining characteristics I hope you and I will be remembered for is generosity. My hope is that people would say of us, "He was defined by generosity" or "She lived what Jesus taught: 'It is more blessed to give than to receive' " (Acts 20:35). My hope is that we would learn the truth of the old saying that is sometimes attributed to Winston Churchill: "We make a living by what we get, but we make a life by what we give."

CREATED TO GIVE, TEMPTED TO KEEP

When God created humankind, God designed us to be generous. God created us with the willingness to give—to God and to others. This design is part of our makeup; we actually have the need to be generous. Yet there are two "voices" that war against our God-given impulse toward generosity, tempting us to keep or hoard what we have.

The first voice is the voice of fear, which tells us, *If you give, there may not be enough left over for you.* We are afraid to be generous because we are afraid of what might happen to us. *What if we don't have enough to fill the gas tank or buy groceries or pay the bills?* Fear, along with a misplaced idea about the true source of our security, keeps us from being generous and leads us to hoard what we have. Yet the truth is that hoarding offers us no real security in this world.

There was a man who gave millions to establish a university in Texas. Several years later he lost nearly everything. Someone asked him if he regretted giving all he had given to the university. His response was telling. "Regret it?" he said, "Look, that school is the only lasting thing I've done with my money. Had I not given for the school, I would have lost that money too, and there would be nothing to show for it."

This man knew that we were created to give, not to hoard. He knew that hoarding his money not only would have been futile; it would have been fruitless.

The second voice is the voice of self-gratification, which tells us, *If you give, you won't have enough money to buy the stuff you need to make you happy.* Our culture tells us that our lives consist in the abundance of our possessions and pleasurable experiences. So we find ourselves thinking, *If I give, there won't be enough left for me.* We do the math and realize that 10 percent of our income could buy a new car or a bigger house—or whatever else we may have our eyes set on. Before long we have convinced ourselves that we need those things if we are going to be truly happy. After all, we don't want to "miss out" on something in life. But as we discussed in the previous chapter, there comes a point when an increasing amount of stuff produces a diminishing return of happiness and satisfaction.

So, how do we defeat the voices of fear and self-gratification? In a sense, they are defeated the moment we put our faith in Jesus Christ. When we give our lives to Christ, invite him to be Lord, and allow the Holy Spirit to begin changing us from the inside out, we find that our fears begin to dissipate and our aim in life shifts from seeking personal pleasure to pleasing God and caring for others. Although we still may wrestle with the voices from time to time, we are able to silence them more readily and effectively the more we grow in Christ. And the more we grow in Christ, the more generous we become, because generosity is a fruit of spiritual growth. Our giving—both to God and to others—is actually a measure of spiritual growth, because giving requires that we trust God to supply our needs.

One of the ways we can cultivate spiritual growth, and subsequently grow in generosity, is to realize that our entire lives belong to the Lord. In my own experience, I have found that this simple prayer helps me commit all of my life to Christ:

I am no longer my own, but thine.
Put me to what thou wilt, rank me with whom thou wilt;
Put me to doing, put me to suffering;
Let me be employed for thee or laid aside for thee,
Exalted for thee or brought low for thee;
Let me be full, let me be empty;
Let me have all things, let me have nothing;
I freely and heartily yield all things to thy pleasure and
    disposal. . . . Amen.[1]

If you will pray this prayer on a regular basis, you will realize that your life is not your own. You will find that you are willing to give more generously and to do things that are a bit risky or that require sacrifice because you know your security is not in your savings account or IRA but in God.

Those who are generous are blessed,
for they share their bread with the poor.
(Proverbs 22:9)

A THEOLOGICAL FOUNDATION FOR GENEROSITY

As the Holy Spirit continues to work in our lives, we begin to think less about ourselves and more about others. We begin to see the needs of others and wonder, *If I don't do something, who will?* As this change takes place within us, we experience real joy. We discover that we find more joy in doing things for other people and for God than we ever did in doing things for ourselves. This is what Jesus meant when he said, "It is more blessed to give than to receive" (Acts 20:35). In the very act of losing our lives, we find life, just as Jesus said, "For those who want to save their life will lose it, and those who lose their life for my sake will find it" (Matthew 16:25).

These spiritual realizations bring us to a central theological foundation for generosity:

Life is a gift, and everything belongs to God.

Even your capacity to acquire wealth is a gift from God. You didn't bring any of it with you when you came into this world, and you won't take any of it with you when you leave. In his wonderful book *When the Game Is Over, It All Goes Back in the Box*, John Ortberg says that at the end of our lives, everything goes back in the box—a box about six-and-a-half feet long by two feet wide, to be exact. We're not taking it with us, so what does it mean to own things? Actually, we don't really own anything. God owns it all. As the psalmist wrote, "The earth is the LORD's and all that is in it" (Psalm 24:1).

God says it this way in the book of Leviticus: "The land is mine...you are but aliens and tenants" (25:23). Isn't that interesting? We are tenants on God's land. We are managers of God's resources—both the natural resources of our planet and the things that we have. In the Book of Genesis, God created Adam and Eve, put them in the midst of the garden, and said, "Now, be fruitful and multiply and oversee this planet. It's mine, and I'm asking you to take care of it on my behalf" (Genesis 1:28, author's paraphrase). We are stewards of the blessings of God, and our goal is to determine what God wants us to do with the resources we have at our disposal.

Obviously, many of our resources go to take care of our needs. Certainly God expects us to have shelter and to eat and to take care of our children. So a large portion of what we have is to be used for those things. God also wants us to enjoy our lives, not to live in poverty. Nevertheless, God expects us to do more than focus only on ourselves. So the Scriptures teach us that we are to help the poor and give to those in need; and when we do, we are blessed. The Scriptures also teach us that we are to return a portion of our livelihood to God.

> *In all this I have given you an example that*
> *by such work we must support the weak,*
> *remembering the words of the Lord Jesus,*
> *for he himself said, "It is more blessed*
> *to give than to receive." (Acts 20:35)*

GIVING TO GOD

From the early days of the Old Testament, God's people observed the practice of giving some portion of the best of what they had to God. In the beginning, the practice was to burn these offerings completely, saving no portion of the offering for food for themselves or others. This was a way of saying, "God, I give this to you, and it's all yours." In later times, the people would bring their offerings to the priests and offer them to God for the work of the temple and the priesthood.

A gift offered to God was called the first fruits or the tithe, and it equaled one-tenth of one's flocks or crops or income. Abraham was the first to give a tithe or tenth. After victory in battle, Abraham took 10 percent of the spoils of war and gave them to the priest-king Melchizedek for God's glory (Genesis 14:17-24). Abraham's grandson, Jacob, whose name also was Israel, made a covenant with God that included giving one-tenth of all he had to God. He said:

> If God will be with me, and will keep me in this way that I go, and will give me bread to eat and clothing to wear, so that I come again to my father's house in peace, then the Lord shall be my God, and this stone, which I have set up for a pillar, shall be God's house; and of all that you give me I will surely give one-tenth to you.
>
> (Genesis 28:20-22)

In the time of Moses, the tithe was codified in the law. God claimed one-tenth of the best the people had. Before giving to the poor and taking care of themselves, they were to bring one-tenth of their first fruits to God. Leviticus 27:30 says, "All tithes from the land, whether the seed from the ground or the fruit from the tree, are the LORD's; they are holy to the LORD." Whether it was the produce of the ground or the offspring of the flocks, the first tenth was holy to the Lord.

Giving a Tithe

As Christians who live under the new covenant, we know that we are not bound by the law of Moses. Rather, we look to it as a guide. What, then, does God expect of us today regarding the tithe? Most Christians agree that the tithe is still a good guideline for our lives, and one that is pleasing to God. We give our tithes to the church to accomplish the work of God's kingdom through the body of Christ, and the church is responsible for praying and discerning how God wants these resources to be used.

Still, tithing can be a challenging idea for many of us. It can be a stretch, especially for those who are wrestling with the voices of fear and self-gratification. David Slagle, pastor of Veritas Church in Decatur, Georgia, uses apples to illustrate this struggle. He invites us to imagine that God has given us ten apples, which represent our wealth or income. God tells us that nine of these apples are ours to enjoy. We are to use some to care for ourselves and for our families, some to save for retirement, and some to give away to others. But the tenth apple is holy to God. Giving this apple to God first, before we consume the other nine apples, is a way for us to express praise, love, obedience, faithfulness, worship, and devotion to God. This also serves to supply the resources for God's purposes to be accomplished in the world through God's church.

Slagle then notes that our lifestyles are such that, for many of us, nine apples are not enough anymore. We think, *How can I pay the bills and have all the stuff I want with just nine apples?* So we decide the Lord will not mind if we take just a little bite of his apple. After all, there's that trip we want to take, and it's really important. So we take a bite out of God's apple—the one that is holy to God and meant to be used for God's purposes. *The Lord will understand,* we think. Then Christmas comes and we don't have enough money for all the presents we want to buy, so we take another bite out of God's apple. One day a medical emergency catches us by surprise. Because we didn't set aside money in an emergency fund, we must take another bite from God's apple. Buying a new car, eating out, spending on this or that—each expense takes a bite out of the apple that belongs to God. Soon all that is left is the core. So we give the core to God and say, "Here's your portion, Lord." God receives not our first fruits or our best gifts, but our leftovers.

I wonder if God must think, *You would really bless me if you recognized that this apple is mine and gave it to me freely—not because someone made you feel guilty, but just because you love me.* You know, a strange thing happens when we give the first apple to God. We are not tempted to eat it, because it's not there! And with God's help, we somehow find a way to make the other nine apples meet our needs.

I realize that it is challenging to tithe. It simply might not be possible for you to begin giving 10 percent to God right away. But I encourage you to take a step in that direction. Perhaps you can give 2 percent or 5 percent or 7 percent. God understands where you are, and God will help you make the adjustments necessary for you to become more and more generous.

Jesus saw a widow who gave her last two copper coins, and he said, "This poor widow has put in more than all those who are contributing to the treasury. For all of them have contributed out of their abundance; but she out of her poverty has put in everything she had, all she had to live on" (Mark 12:43-44). The Lord understands your situation and is pleased when you give freely with a grateful heart. The Lord also is ready to help you make the changes in your lifestyle that will enable you to tithe.

Contrary to popular belief, tithing is possible at virtually any income level. I know this is true from personal experience. The first year LaVon and I were married, we lived just below the poverty level for a family of two, yet we gave God a tenth of what we had before we spent anything on ourselves. When I was in college and seminary, we lived hand to mouth and paycheck to paycheck. We would get to the end of every pay period and have a negative balance in the checkbook register, yet we always gave our first tenth to the Lord. It was hard. Yet nothing was ever repossessed, and somehow we were always okay. In fact, we were more than okay. We were blessed.

There are different opinions regarding whether the tithe should be calculated on gross or net income. The formula LaVon and I have always used to calculate our tithe is based on net income. We subtract Social Security because we will pay tithes on these monies when we receive them. We subtract taxes because we do not actually see this money and because we view this amount as the price of doing business here in America. If we receive a refund on our taxes, however, we do tithe on this amount.

As our income has grown through the years, it would be easy for our family to look at our tithe and think, *That's a lot of money; does God really mean 10 percent of that?* I recall a story told by Peter Marshall, who was chaplain of the United States Senate for many years. There was a man who struggled to tithe even though he had a large income. The man said to Marshall, "I have a problem. I used to tithe regularly some years ago, but...but now...I am earning $500,000 a year, and there is just no way I can afford to give about $50,000."

Marshall reflected on this wealthy man's dilemma but gave no advice. He simply said, "I can certainly see your problem. Let's pray about it." The man agreed. So Marshall bowed his head and prayed with boldness and authority, "Heavenly Father, I pray that you would reduce this man's salary back to the place that he can afford to tithe."[2]

Our thinking seems to change as we make more money, doesn't it? According to Forbes' annual survey in 2017, there are 2,043 billionaires in the world, more than twice as many as there were just a decade ago.[3] Yet the percentage of giving among the majority of these billionaires does not rise above the single digits. How can you be a billionaire and give away such a small percentage of your income? Do you need the rest of it "just in case"? Or is there really that much stuff you can spend your money on? The truth is that regardless of our income level, each of us is faced with the same question: How many apples are enough? As nine apples grow to twenty apples, to forty apples, and more, we basically have two choices: Store them in storehouses, or share them with others.

> *"From everyone to whom much has been given, much will be required; and from the one to whom much has been entrusted, even more will be demanded." (Luke 12:48)*

Giving Beyond the Tithe

We who are blessed with more than enough apples to meet our needs should come to a place where we are able to say, *I have more apples than I can use. I'm going to give away this apple to the poor. And maybe I can give away another apple to an organization that is doing God's work and changing the world.* This is when we begin to understand what Jesus meant when he said, "To whom much has been given, much will be required" (Luke 12:48).

This truth became very real to me several years ago as LaVon and I came to realize that tithing is a floor, not a ceiling. God calls us to grow beyond the tithe. So, as I mentioned in chapter 2, we made it a goal to give away an increasing amount of our income each year. After tithing 10 percent, we set aside an additional percentage of our income as offerings for other things that are important to us. Through the years, we have given these offerings to church building funds, mission projects, schools, and other nonprofit organizations. We truly enjoy having money that is designated for giving; it is a source of great joy to us. Although we were unable to set aside a definite percentage above the tithe for giving when we were younger, even in the years when we were struggling to make ends meet we managed to sponsor children in other countries and give to various causes. So, I encourage you to consider not only tithing but also going beyond the tithe as you are able.

Our tithes and offerings are a tangible sign of our desire to live wholly for God. They are an expression of gratitude, worship, and praise. They demonstrate that we put God first in our lives. They are an investment in God's work through the church. And, without a doubt, they are pleasing to God.

> *"Truly I tell you, just as you did it to one of the least of these who are members of my family, you did it to me." (Matthew 25:40)*

WHAT OUR GENEROSITY MEANS TO GOD

I once did a study of the practice of worship in the Bible. I searched every passage of Scripture where people worshipped God, capturing 1,600 years of biblical history. I was surprised by what I found. From the earliest biblical times, the primary way people worshipped God was not by singing songs of praise or listening to sermons. The central act of worship was building an altar and offering the fruit of one's labors upon it to God. As I've mentioned, they would burn the sacrifice of an animal or grain as a way of expressing their gratitude, devotion, and desire to honor God. The scent of the offering was said to be pleasing to God. It wasn't that God loved the smell of burnt meat and grain. Rather, God saw that people were giving a gift that expressed love, faith, and the desire to please and honor God, and this moved God's heart.

Eight or nine years ago, our family took a camping trip to the Grand Tetons. We arrived on my birthday and set up our little pop-up camper. After we were settled, we told each of our daughters that they could have $20 spending money for the three days we would be in and around Jackson Hole. We then went to the gift shop before heading out on a walk around a small lake. We had no sooner walked into the gift shop than Rebecca started looking at ball caps. She found one, tried it on, and said, "Dad, what do you think of this hat?" I said, "Becca, it's really cool. But all you have is $20, and that hat will take all of your money. Why don't you wait and make your money last for the next few days." But she said, "Dad, you told me it was my money and I could get whatever I want. And I really want this hat!" As hard as I tried to talk her out of it, and to convince her that she would have other opportunities to buy a cap in town, she would have no part of waiting. Finally, exasperated, I said, "Okay, Becca—but this is it. You're not getting any more money the next three days." I gave her her $20, and she bought the hat.

We went for a walk around the lake, and then came back to watch the sun set from a park bench. That's when Becca handed me the hat and said, "Daddy, I bought this for you. I love you. Happy birthday." I sat on the bench, took her in my arms, and started to cry. That hat is among my most treasured possessions, my most often worn hat to this day because every time I wear it, I think of Becca's sacrifice for me. All these years later it still touches me to think about how my little girl gave up all her spending money because she wanted to tell her daddy that she loved him.

That's how God looks at your offerings. They are not financial transactions or business deals. Your offerings are a way of saying, "God, I'm returning to you a portion of what I have and what I've earned to say thank you and I love you. I hope you'll use this somehow to make a difference in the world."

Becca didn't give me the hat to get something from me. There was something in her heart that prompted her to give up her spending money for her dad, and that something was pure, selfless love. Our offerings, when given to God in this same spirit, are received by God in this way. They bless the Lord.

WHAT HAPPENS WHEN WE ARE GENEROUS

Our generosity to God and others not only touches God and other people, it also changes us. As human beings, we were created with the need to be generous. When we are not generous in giving of what we have, we have not only a financial problem but also a spiritual problem. To use a somewhat graphic yet extremely effective analogy, it is as if we have become financially and spiritually constipated. We keep taking in, but we're not giving out. After a while, it becomes uncomfortable and causes us pain. Sometimes we may not even realize what is happening. We're taking in, but it is not satisfying us because we were not made to take in and never give anything back. We were created for generosity. Over time we become self-absorbed, money-consumed, joyless people. This is what a lifetime of financial and spiritual constipation looks like: joylessness.

The only way to find relief is to learn to give. When we are generous—to God and to our families, friends, neighbors, and others who are in need—our hearts are filled with joy. They are enlarged by the very act of giving. When we give generously, we become more generous. That is how generosity works.

In the beginning, we may be hesitantly generous. We may be reluctant. But something happens to us in the midst of our giving, and we find ourselves becoming more generous. In this respect, generosity is similar to love and gratitude. Sometimes we may not feel love, but when we choose to act in loving ways, loving feelings begin to flow. Sometimes we may not feel like giving thanks, but the best way to cultivate a heart of gratitude is to give thanks in all circumstances. Likewise, the more we give, the more generous our hearts become.

> *Each of you must give as you have made*
> *up your mind, not reluctantly or under*
> *compulsion, for God loves a cheerful giver.*
> *(2 Corinthians 9:7)*

Generosity changes us, filling us with joy and filling our lives with blessings. When we are generous with what we have, we find that unexpected blessings flow back into our lives, catching us by surprise. Somewhere along the way, as we see our acts of generosity helping others and perhaps even changing the world, we say in wonder and amazement, "Wow, look what happened," and we find ourselves blessed. What's more, as our generosity blesses others, they are changed, too.

Jeff Hanson is a fifteen-year-old student at the Kansas School for the Blind. He is visually impaired as the result of an optic nerve tumor caused by a genetic condition called neurofibromatosis. Thanks to chemotherapy and other treatments, he is doing well. With his glasses, he can now see the big "E" on the top of the eye chart. Jeff is a gifted young man. He bakes and paints, sells his creations, and donates the money to the Children's Tumor Foundation (www.jeffreyowenhanson. com/). So far he has given over $15,000 to this foundation. He also gives of his time to bless others in service.

In the fall of 2005, when he was receiving chemotherapy, Jeff was granted a wish by the Make-A-Wish Foundation. His wish was to meet Elton John. When Elton announced that he was coming to town for a concert, Make-A-Wish contacted Jeff to say that he would get to meet Elton backstage before the concert.

The day arrived, and Elton met Jeff backstage before the show. Elton was gracious and generous with his time. Jeff told Elton his story and gave him a package of note cards with his paintings on the fronts. Then, before saying good-bye, Jeff reached in his pocket and pulled out a check for $1,000 for the Elton John AIDS Foundation.

Jeff Hanson, twelve years old at the time, gave a thousand-dollar check to Elton John. My guess is that Elton was virtually speechless. Elton had wanted to bless Jeff, but now he was the one who was being blessed. No doubt he was touched and perhaps changed in some way by Jeff's generosity. So he asked the photographer to capture the moment with a picture. A week later the Children's Tumor Foundation called Jeff to tell him they had just received a $5,000 check in the mail from Elton John in honor of Jeff.

But there's more to the story. Before Elton and Jeff's visit was over on the day of the concert, Elton asked Jeff if he had ever been to Dubai. When Jeff said no, Elton invited to fly Jeff and his parents to Dubai for an all-expenses-paid stay while he was in concert there. He explained that he wanted to hear more about Jeff's work.

Even at his young age, Jeff Hanson understands what life is really about. Though he could feel sorry for himself, he has chosen to focus his attention on helping others. In the process, others have been changed. Other people have become more generous. Jeff's generosity has returned to be a blessing to him. I believe this is what Jesus had in mind when he said, "Give, and it will be given to you. A good measure, pressed down, shaken together, running over, will be put into your lap; for the measure you give will be the measure you get back" (Luke 6:38). God says it this way in Malachi 3:10: "Bring the full tithe into the storehouse, so that there may be food in my house, and thus put me to the test, says the LORD of hosts; see if I will not open the windows of heaven for you and pour down for you an overflowing blessing."

Many Christians have it wrong. They say that if you give, then God will give more back to you. But that is not how it works. We do not give to God so that we can get something in return. But when we give to God and to others, the blessings seem to come back to us. Of course, there is no guarantee that if you tithe you will never lose your job or never have other bad things happen to you. Nevertheless, when we give generously, the unmistakable blessings of God flow into our lives.

Let us take God at his word. As we choose to live for others and to give generously of what God has given us, we will both bless others and experience the abundant blessings that come from living for God.

THINKING IT THROUGH

- Read Acts 4:32-35. How was the church in Acts defined by generosity? What ways would your life change if you were defined by generosity?

- Read Matthew 25:14-21. Like the master, God has given us things in life that we are "in charge of." What has God put you "in charge of" in your life, and how are you managing it?

- Read Mark 12:41-44. What does it mean to give sacrificially? Has anyone ever sacrificed something so that you could have something? What was that like for you? How has this generous person affected your own vision of what matters in life?

- Read Matthew 25:34-40. One motivation to be generous is to think the person may be Christ. What moves you or motivates you to be generous?

- Read Luke 19:1-10. How did Jesus demonstrate generosity to Zacchaeus? What did Zacchaeus do in response? When have you been changed by someone else's generosity toward you? When have you given something that brought you great joy?

- Read Luke 12:41-48. How much do you believe you have been given? How close are you to doing all that you can do with what you have been given? What practical steps can you take to increase your generosity in the next twelve months?

EPILOGUE

LIVING THE GOOD LIFE

LIVING THE GOOD LIFE

*One of them, a lawyer, asked him a question
to test him. "Teacher, which commandment in the law
is the greatest?" He said to him, "'You shall love the
Lord your God with all your heart, and with all your
soul, and with all your mind.' This is the greatest and
first commandment. And a second is like it: 'You shall
love your neighbor as yourself.' On these two
commandments hang all the law and the prophets."
(Matthew 22:35-40)*

*I trusted in your steadfast love;
my heart shall rejoice in your salvation.
I will sing to the LORD,
because he has dealt bountifully with me.
(Psalm 13:5-6)*

Nobody says, "Give me the mediocre life. Give me the lousy life." Everybody wants to experience the good life. Going back to the ancient Greeks, philosophers have argued that the good life should be our aim. Hedonism was the philosophical school that articulated this view. Hedonists believed that the chief purpose of human life is to experience as much pleasure as possible and to minimize pain.

Today it is widely accepted in our culture that pleasure is the path to the good life. There also is a common assumption that if you can accumulate material possessions, if you have enough wealth, and if you can save enough for retirement, you will experience the good life that everyone wants.

My wife makes delicious chocolate chip cookies, and I love eating them when they are warm, just out of the oven. The first three or four are delicious. But the more I eat, the less I enjoy them. And if I eat a dozen warm cookies, rather than feeling satisfied, I'll actually feel sick to my stomach. In the same way, a focus on the acquisition of more money and possessions does not lead to satisfaction; sometimes it just leaves us feeling sick.

The writer of the Book of Ecclesiastes in the Old Testament, who identifies himself simply as the Teacher, understood this. As he looked back on his life, the Teacher explained that he had tried to fill his life with every pleasurable experience. Only afterward did he realize that it was all meaningless. He had been "chasing after wind" (2:11).

It seems that people today continue to miss this lesson. I read about a recent study involving 120 people who, on average, earned $25 million per year. These multimillionaires were asked questions about such things as whether they thought they had enough, if they felt secure, and if they were experiencing the good life based upon their standards of living. The consistent answer to these questions was no.[1]

Next, the millionaires were asked, "How much more income would you need to have in order to feel like you were secure?" And the average answer was that if they could have 25 percent more—which works out to about $6.25 million more each year—they would finally feel secure and satisfied.

For those of us who don't have annual incomes in the millions, the answers in this survey may seem absurd. We would enjoy the challenge of finding satisfaction on a $25 million annual budget. But that's just chasing after the wind on a bigger scale.

THE UNHAPPINESS REPORT

As we look back on the past fifty years in the United States, in much the same way the Teacher in Ecclesiastes reflected on his own experience, we can see what has happened when people have tried the counterfeit path to the good life. During the past five decades, the gross domestic product of the United States per person has roughly increased by a factor of two. Americans' standard of living has gone up dramatically. The average new home fifty years ago was one-third the size of an average new home today. Yet studies say that we are actually three percent less happy than we were fifty years ago. Clearly, having more wealth and more possessions hasn't led to more satisfaction in our lives.

Every year since 2012, the United Nations has issued a study called the "World Happiness Report." They survey thousands of people in fifty different countries, attempting to find out how happy people are in those countries and what factors make them happy. In that very first report, the United States ranked twenty-third. In terms of overall happiness with their lives, the people of the wealthiest nation in the world ranked behind a number of much less prosperous nations, including Malaysia, Tanzania, Indonesia, Andorra, Thailand, Vietnam, and El Salvador.[2] In subsequent years the United States has moved up a few spots in the happiness rankings, but we're still nowhere near the top.

In 2016 I read an article written by a very successful entrepreneur and was struck by what she said: "At the height of my success I was actually pretty miserable. I'm not saying there's an inverse relationship between success and happiness, just that there's not necessarily a positive one. They are two very different things."[3] Achieving success is not the same as achieving happiness or experiencing the good life.

I think of another story I heard several years ago about a group of mountain climbers. This particular group had spent years preparing for the adventure. On their way up, they encountered the kind of terrible, sudden snowstorm that is common on some of the world's greatest mountain peaks. As the team ascended the mountain, some of the members died. The remaining members pushed on to the peak. When they made it to the summit, the leader of the expedition stood looking around. All he could think about was the cost of the expedition, how many years and how much money they had invested in the trip, and how some of their friends had perished. Standing there at the peak, he asked himself, "Is this all? Is this really all there is?"

What do you do when you reach the top of the world and find you've been chasing after the wind? Where do we turn after we realize that success is not the same as happiness?

GOING FOR EUDAIMONIA

Maybe we need to redefine what the good life means.

For that, we can turn to a Greek word, *eudaimonia*. If you've studied philosophy, you may remember this word, which was popularized by Aristotle. The word means joy and happiness, but it doesn't define these qualities only in terms of wealth or success. A better way to understand *eudaimonia* is as "human flourishing." As Aristotle used it, the term meant "the highest human good"—what we might in fact call the good life, not just for ourselves but for others, too.

So, how do we flourish as human beings? Earlier in this book I talked about some of the keys to the good life as they relate to money and possessions.

One key is to cultivate gratitude. Be grateful for what we have.

Another key is to pursue a purpose bigger than ourselves.

A third key is to live beneath our means. This gives us the margin to have "enough," to de-stress, to save and give.

And, of course, a fourth key is to apply Jesus' teaching that it is better to give than to receive—to be generous toward family, friends, and causes that matter to you, and toward God.

These four keys can serve as markers on the pathway to true happiness and satisfaction. But where does the pathway lead? How do we find our way to the good life?

INVESTING IN RELATIONSHIPS

One pathway to the good life is investing in people and relationships. This is taught in the Bible, but also by Greek and Roman philosophers as well as modern-day positive psychologists. They all stack hands on the truth that we experience the good life in our relationships with those closest to us and with our fellow human beings.

The United Nations' "World Happiness Report," mentioned earlier, actually uses that Greek word, *eudaimonia*, and connects it to living in accord with what is intrinsically worthwhile and meaningful to human beings. The happiness index used by the United Nations includes a sense of purpose, meaningful relationships, good health, and contribution to the community. As the report says, "Human beings are social animals. We are happier when we are with others and our most rewarding experiences are normally connected with human relationships."[4]

Isn't that interesting? Scientific research confirms what the Bible has always taught us.

But what the Bible teaches contradicts with what many of us learn from our own culture. We graduate high school or college and begin our career with a drive to succeed, based on what we have learned from our society. We may establish certain career goals for ourselves—and then we keep raising the bar as we meet those goals. We've been acculturated to the idea that attaining those goals will bring us the good life.

In the process, though, we forget the lessons from the Teacher in Ecclesiastes. We forget that Jesus urged us not to worry about our material possessions:

> "Consider the lilies of the field, how they grow; they neither toil nor spin, yet I tell you, even Solomon in all his glory was not clothed like one of these."

> (Matthew 6:28-29)

We forget that the secrets of the good life are literally all around us in the relationships we have with other people.

Jrue Holiday is a remarkable man who plays point guard for the NBA New Orleans Pelicans. Through his first eight seasons after entering the league in 2009, Jrue was averaging better than 14 points per game.[5] Lots of teams would be interested in having him play for them. Jrue's wife, Lauren, is a great athlete, too. And in her own field, like Jrue, she had risen to the top of her sport; for eight years, she played midfielder for the U.S. women's national soccer team.

In the summer of 2016, when Lauren was about five months pregnant, she was diagnosed with a brain tumor. At that point Jrue contacted the management of the Pelicans. Even with his whole career ahead of Jrue felt that "nothing comes before my daughter and my wife. I knew that the best thing for me to do was to be with my family, help my wife through this hard time as best as possible ... try to be there for her as best as I could."

The team, understandably, didn't want Jrue to quit. Instead, they gave him an indefinite leave of absence. They told him he could come back and his spot would be waiting for him. But first he could make sure that Lauren, whom Jrue calls "my number one teammate," was healthy again.[6]

In September 2016, the Holidays' daughter, named Jrue for her father, was born. The next month, Lauren underwent successful surgery to remove the tumor. Jrue returned to the Pelicans; since then, the team has signed him to a new, long-term contract.

Not everyone can quit their job if a spouse becomes sick. Not everyone earns enough that they can afford to take a break. Even so, the time may come when we have to reorder our priorities and ask, "What really matters in my life?" And at even at those times—maybe especially at those times—we may find that what brings us happiness are the relationships we have with people.

Wall Street was a little shaken in 2016 when Charles W. Sharf announced his resignation as CEO of Visa, the credit card company. He'd been in that role for four years. During his tenure, the stock price of Visa had risen by 134 percent. He was at the pinnacle of success, and the future was wide open for him. Everybody asked why he was quitting. And his answer was simple: His wife and kids lived on the East Coast, and his office with Visa was on the West Coast. He wanted to make sure he got to spend time with them.

Most of us can't step away from work, even if we have a sick spouse or a family that lives across the country. But most of us understand the struggle in finding a balance between career and family. I have known this challenge, and I didn't even know I was struggling. When I was assigned to start the United Methodist Church of the Resurrection in 1990, I was twenty-five years old and driven to help the church become everything it could be. For years this meant I was away from home six nights a week. It meant being gone much of the day on Saturday and Sunday and missing lots and lots of soccer games and softball games and swim meets. And I didn't think I was chasing success. I never had visions of church membership in the thousands; I just wanted us to do great ministry. But I *was* driven, and in the midst of my drivenness I missed out on many things with my children that I now regret missing.

The relationships that help us find the good life go beyond children and family. They also involve friends and the people we surround ourselves with. As I can state from experience, those other relationships become particularly important as time goes by. A few years ago, LaVon and I started a small group at the church; the group gave us the chance to connect with twelve people and build friendships with them. They became the people we "did life" with. We've gone on mission trips with them and taken vacations together. We've spent many evenings on our screened-in porch with them, just chatting and sharing pizza. Our times together have been some of the happiest in my life. I'm so glad that, after time with our children, this group became a priority in our lives.

Because relationships matter so much, I recommend if you have the opportunity that you get involved with other Christians in a small group, Sunday school class, Bible study, home group, men's or women's group, or youth group. I believe you'll find that the relationships you form there will deepen and strengthen your faith and will make you a happier, healthier person.

LIVING FOR OTHERS

Another pathway to the good life also involves relationships, but it goes beyond the close relationships we have with family and friends; rather, it has to do with how we live our lives in relation to the world around us—particularly to people whom we're called to bless, to stand with, and to advocate for. To be a part of the human community, seeking the good of all, is actually a driver of happiness in our own lives. As we've learned, God told Abraham not merely that he was being blessed, but that God had blessed him so he might be a blessing to others.

God created us to be authentically human, and to do so means to bless other people, to care about other human beings, to work for the common good. As Martin Luther King Jr. said, "We are prone to judge success by the index of our salaries or the size of our automobiles, rather than by the quality of our service and relationship to humanity."[7] He understood that the true measure of success is the quality of our relationships with other human beings. Albert Einstein meant much the same thing when he said: "Try not to become a man of success but rather try to become a man of value."[8]

Our ultimate example, of course, is Jesus. On the night before he died, Jesus shocked his disciples by washing their feet, one of the humblest tasks anyone in his day could perform. It was a dramatic illustration of his teaching: "Whoever wants to be first must be last of all and servant of all" (Mark 9:35). And then the next day, in his single greatest act, Jesus laid down his life to redeem the human race.

Here's what Jesus—in fact, the entirety of Scripture— consistently teaches us: The life that God wants for us, the good life, is lived in relationship to other people. The prophet Micah asks what the Lord requires of us, and then he provides the answer: "To do justice, and to love kindness, and to walk humbly with your God" (Micah 6:8).

When Jesus was asked about the greatest commandment, he cited two:

> " 'You shall love the Lord your God with all your heart, and with all your soul, and with all your mind.' This is the greatest and first commandment. And a second is like it: 'You shall love your neighbor as yourself.' "
>
> (Matthew 22:37-39)

Everything else, Jesus said, somehow fits into those two commands. Jesus was teaching us that *eudaimonia*, the good life, is found in our love for God and our relationships with one another.

You may notice that the Gospels contain a whole series of "one anothers." Love one another. Serve one another. Bless one another. Forgive one another. Do unto one another. They tell us how the Christian life is lived. They show us that the good life is found in how we treat one another.

That's also one of the messages of 1 John, which describes the good life this way: "We know that we have passed from death to life because we love one another" (1 John 3:14). We see death in this life, but we move from death into the life that God intends for us when we love others, when we care for them, when we bless them, when we seek to serve, when we put the others' needs before our own. When we are doing those things, we live the life of love.

We experience happiness and fulfillment when we live a good life toward other human beings. We receive joy in the giving of ourselves.

THE WAY, THE TRUTH, AND THE GOOD LIFE

There are three different Greek words in the New Testament for *life*, though each has a slightly different meaning. One of the words is *bios*, from which we get our English word *biology*. There's *psuche* or *psyche*, which is the word that's behind *psychology*. And then there's *zoe*, from which we get our word *gy*. Of the three, *zoe* is the word used most often in the New Testament—some 275 times. In my library, I have a Greek dictionary that allows me to see what Greek words meant to people in the time of Paul and in the New Testament context. According to my dictionary, *zoe* meant fullness of life, real life, genuine life—in other words, what we're calling the good life.

And how do we find *zoe*? What is the ultimate pathway to the good life? Jesus tells us in John 14:6: "I am the way, and the truth, and the life [*zoe*]"—in other words, I am the pathway to the true life that you've been longing for and that God wants for you and for everyone.

If we're searching for the good life, the New Testament shouts to us, "Hey, here it is." It's found in trusting in God through Jesus Christ. It's in relationship with God.

The great thing about this picture of the good life is that you can experience it without cramming your life full of pleasures and materials things. You can experience it even when you're living in poverty. You can experience it even when you're going through a divorce, when you've received a difficult diagnosis from the doctor, when you've been devastated by the death of a loved one. When the foundations of your world are shaken, you can still find the good life by trusting in God through Jesus Christ.

At the beginning of this chapter are words from Psalm 13:5-6. The psalmist says,

I trusted in your steadfast love;
    my heart shall rejoice in your salvation.
I will sing to the LORD,
      because he has dealt bountifully with me.

Maybe your first reaction when you read those words is, "Things are going well for this guy. Of course he's going to sing God's praises. Of course he feels like rejoicing. God's been good to him."

But what's fascinating about these lines is that they actually make up the fifth verse in a lament psalm. When you read the earlier verses, you find that things have not been going well at all in the psalmist's life. Here's how Psalm 13 begins:

How long, O LORD? Will you forget me forever?
    How long will you hide your face from me?
How long must I bear pain in my soul,
    and have sorrow in my heart all day long?
How long shall my enemy be exalted over me?

Consider and answer me, O LORD my God!
    Give light to my eyes, or I will sleep the sleep
    of death,
and my enemy will say, "I have prevailed";
    my foes will rejoice because I am shaken.
                    (Psalm 13:1-4)

Then, in the very next verse, the psalmist turns around and sings God's praises. He announces his trust in God's unfailing love. These words remind us to hold tight to God with a dogged determination. They remind us to trust that, no matter what kind of hell we're walking through, God is walking through it with us, and somehow it will be okay. We are going to experience the peace that surpasses all understanding, and that will help guard our hearts and minds. We need not be afraid when we're walking through the valley of the shadow of death. We can know that God is our Redeemer, and because of that we don't have to be afraid. We recognize that nothing can separate us from the love of God. And so we can find ourselves caught up, even in the midst of adversity, into God's good life.

The apostle Paul said it this way: "We are experiencing all kinds of trouble, but we aren't crushed" (2 Corinthians 4:8 CEB). Those are the words of a man who had been imprisoned multiple times. He had been beaten and stoned and ultimately would be killed for his faith. In spite of everything Paul had endured, he went on to tell the Corinthians, "We are confused, but we aren't depressed. We are harassed, but we aren't abandoned. We are knocked down, but we are not knocked out" (verses 8-9). Paul kept faith and had hope. He fixed his eyes, he said, "not on what is seen, but on what is unseen" (verse 18 NIV). When you can experience the good life in the midst of adversity, you know there's something real to the kind of faith that Paul describes.

I've noticed that on mission trips to developing countries, our people frequently comment on how happy the children seem in the midst of poverty. The children have no toys to play with. They have no shoes on their feet. They live in homes with dirt floors. But there's joy in their lives. They have relationships with each other. They trust in God. And they're full of joy.

WHAT SUCCESS LOOKS LIKE

David and Janet Roberts were founding members of Church of the Resurrection. They helped make telephone calls to the community before we even had our very first worship service. I first visited with David and Janet at their home, a small ranch house with a one-car garage. David was a restaurateur for a while, and after his restaurant business failed, he found a job on the night shift at UPS. He gradually worked up to the day shift and moved up from delivering to account management, and finally became a senior account manager for thirteen years. He was highly respected in his workplace. He did an excellent job, but his job was never the most important thing in his life.

David passed away in 2016. The last time I saw him was at one of Kansas City's hospice centers the week before he died. David had graduated from a music conservatory in Kansas City, and he loved to sing. Every year at our Christmas Eve candlelight services, he would sing "O Holy Night." So before I went to visit him, I printed off the words to "O Holy Night" and brought them with me to the hospice. Janet and their two sons, Brice and Cole, were there, and we all sang "O Holy Night" to David as he lay there in his bed.

The next day one of our associate pastors went to call on David, who was close to death. The associate pastor had brought along his hymnal, and he joined Brice, Cole, and Janet at David's bedside, where they had been singing hymns to David all morning. Hymn singing had always been a family tradition.

The associate pastor sat down with Janet and her sons, and they began "Blessed Assurance." They reached the second verse, and when they sang the words "angels descending," David took his last breath. David trusted God all the way to the very end, surrounded by the people he loved.

A few days after his death, I went to the Robertses' home. They still lived in that same ranch house with the one-car garage. Had they wanted, they easily could have moved years earlier into a mini-mansion with a three-car garage in a more expensive neighborhood. But it just wasn't that important to them.

As I sat with Brice and Cole, I asked them to tell me what they would remember most about David. They said, "Our dad was the most amazing father in the whole world. He loved and cared for us and put us first." And then Janet began to tell me about how David had invested twenty-six years of his life in the Boy Scouts at nearby Asbury United Methodist Church, how he had been a beloved mentor to those kids. At David's funeral, I watched as people stood up and shared stories of what he had done for them and others. And I read aloud some stories of people whose lives had been changed by him. When the funeral ended, I looked at the picture of David and thought, "Now, that is what success looks like."

I wonder if you're a success in life. It doesn't have to do with how much money you make, how much pleasure you cram into your life, or what level of achievement you've had with the company. It has everything to do with how you love the people who were put in your path, how you made the world a better place by investing in other human beings, and how you trusted in God's unfailing love. When you do those things, nobody will have to tell you about how to find the good life. You will know for yourself that you are living it.

THINKING IT THROUGH

- Read Isaiah 55:1-3. Where in our society do you see people spending their money for bread that does not satisfy? Where do you see this in your own life?

- Read 1 Corinthians 12:12-26. How does Paul use the parts of the body as a metaphor to explain what kind of relationship God wants us to have with others? Why, by Paul's logic, should all suffer if one member is suffering?

- Read Genesis 1:26-27. What does it mean to be made in God's image? How does being made in God's image provide a basis for the commandment to love our neighbor and find the good life in relationship with our fellow human beings? Now read Isaiah 58:6-12. How does the prophet, speaking for God, describe the nature of true worship? How does this passage depict a vision of the good life?

- Read Luke 11:1-4. How is radical trust reflected in the words of the Lord's Prayer, asking God to "give us each day our daily bread"? What would radical trust mean in your own life?

- Read 1 John 3:11-17 and 4:7-5:4. What do you think it means in 1 John 4:18 to "[reach] perfection in love"? How does love for others take us from death into life? John says not to be astonished that the world would hate us for practicing this kind of self-sacrificing love. Why do you think that would be the case?

FINANCIAL
MANAGEMENT
ASSESSMENT
TOOLS

FINANCIAL MANAGEMENT ASSESSMENT TOOLS

REFLECTING ON THE SIX FINANCIAL PLANNING PRINCIPLES

Review the six financial planning principles, reading the Scripture verse(s) related to each one and answering the questions that follow. This process will help you think through your current situation and begin to identify changes you can make over the next twelve months.

1. Pay your tithe and offering first.
Read 2 Corinthians 9:6-7.

- How much time do you currently devote to Bible study and prayer each week? What are two changes you could make in your weekly routine in order to move into a deeper study and prayer life?

- What percentage of your income currently goes to charitable giving? Are there changes you'd like to make in this area? (Examples: Track your giving more closely; be more aware of how charitable organizations spend your money; consolidate your giving.)

2. Create a budget and track your expenses.
Read Proverbs 27:23-24.

- What things are you doing well in the area of spending? In what ways is your spending off-track?

- What three changes could you make immediately in order to have a positive impact on your spending overall?

- How well are you doing in following a spending plan or budget? (Use the worksheet on page 60 to evaluate your current spending habits and create a budget for the next twelve months.)

3. *Simplify your lifestyle (live below your means).*
   Read Matthew 6:19-33.

   - What financial habits do you need to forgo in order to have money for things that are more important?

   - In what ways do you burn or waste money? What changes can you make so that you may use this money for other things?

4. Establish an emergency fund. Read Proverbs 21:20.

- How much money do you currently have set aside for emergencies?

- How much can you set aside now as a starting balance for an emergency fund? How much can you save each month? How long will it take you to reach the goal of three months' worth of income?

5. Pay off your credit cards, use cash/debit cards for purchases, and use credit wisely. Read Proverbs 22:7.

- What is your total debt? (Include credit cards, mortgage, second mortgage, home equity loans, car loans, student loans, and so forth.)

- How would you like to change your personal debt situation over the next five to ten years?

6. *Practice long-term savings and investing habits. Read 1 Timothy 6:9-12 and Luke 14:28.*

    - What is the current amount of your savings? (Include personal savings accounts, money market accounts, CDs, mutual funds, pension funds, 401(k) plans, and so forth.)

    - How can you change your savings habits today and move toward security and fulfillment in the future?

14 FINANCIAL MANAGEMENT TIPS

1. Develop a spending plan.

2. Reduce your spending.

3. Pay down your debt. Make it your goal to eliminate consumer debt. Use a timeline of months, years.

4. Stop using credit cards; if you must use credit, use only one card.

5. Pay off credit card balances each month.

6. Find ways to earn more money.

7. Communicate clearly with your creditors.

8. Find a financial coach to help you do a financial assessment, spending plan, and develop your financial goals. Consider and compare certified credit counselor agencies (www.usdoj.gov/ust, www.fcaa.org/, or https://www.nfcc.org/).

9. If you apply for a debt consolidation loan (second mortgage), make sure your new monthly payment is much lower and that you can make such payments.

10. Borrowing from a friend or family member should be the last resort. Do not ask someone to cosign on a loan.

11. Check your credit report each year for errors, at www.annualcreditreport.com.

12. Establish an emergency fund.

13. Protect your family with insurance: Term Life, Health Care, Disability, Auto, and Homeowners.

14. Buy your home.

CREDIT CARD PAY-OFF STRATEGY

Use this technique to pay off multiple credit card balances. This method is simple and effective.

Review your credit card situation:
- Which cards have the highest balances?
- Which cards have the highest interest rates?

1. Start with the card that has the lowest balance.

Determine the amount you can pay each month over the minimum payment in order to completely eliminate this debt. Be aggressive, pay it off, and celebrate when it is paid.

Pay off the card according to your plan.

2. Next, move to the card with the next lowest balance.

Apply the same amount you paid on the first card payment plus the minimum required and eliminate that credit card debt.

Pay off the card according to your plan.

3. Continue to pay off each credit card in this way, one at a time, until they are all paid off. By using the determined amount plus the minimum you can become debt free.

Note: If two cards have the same balance, pay off the card with the highest interest rate first.

NOTES

Introduction: The Courage to Be Free and Bear Fruit

1. "A Look at the Shocking Student Loan Debt Statistics for 2017," Student Loan Hero, September 13, 2017, https://studentloanhero. com/student-loan-debt-statistics/, accessed December 14, 2017.

2. Jessica Dickler, "US households now have over $16,000 in credit-card debt," CNBC, December 13, 2016, https://www.cnbc.com/2016/12 /13/us-households-now-have-over-16k-in-credit-card-debt.html, accessed December 14, 2017.

3. "Household Expenditures and Income: Balancing Family Finances in Today's Economy," The Pew Charitable Trust, March 30, 2016, http://www.pewtrusts.org/en/research-and-analysis/issue-briefs /2016/03/household-expenditures-and-income, accessed December 14, 2017.

4. Phil LeBeau, "New car, new reality: Auto loan borrowing hits fresh highs," CNBC, June 2, 2016, https://www.cnbc.com/2016/06/02 /us-borrowers-are-paying-more-and-for-longer-on-their-auto-loans. html, accessed December 14, 2017.

5. Kathleen Elkins, "Here's how much the average family has saved for retirement at every age," CNBC, April 7, 2017, https://www.cnbc .com/2017/04/07/how-much-the-average-family-has-saved-for -retirement-at-every-age.html, accessed December 14, 2017.

6. Justin McCarthy, "Americans' Financial Worries Edge Up in 2016," Gallup News, April 28, 2016, http://news.gallup.com/poll/191174 /americans-financial-worries-edge-2016.aspx, accessed December 14, 2017.

7.   Jessica Dickler, "No. 1 cause of money stress: When expenses exceed income," CNBC, June 27, 2017, https://www.cnbc.com/2017/06/26/greatest-cause-of-money-stress-when-expenses-exceed-income.html, accessed December 14, 2017.

8.   "Divorce Study: Financial Arguments Early in Relationship May Predict Divorce," *Huffington Post*, July 12, 2013, https://www.huffingtonpost.com/2013/07/12/divorce-study_n_3587811.html, accessed December 14, 2017.

9.   *The New American Standard New Testament Greek Lexicon*, s.v. "Metanoia," https://www.biblestudytools.com/lexicons/greek/nas/metanoia.html, accessed December 14, 2017.

Chapter 1: When Dreams Become Nightmares

1.   "Dog Offered Credit Card," BBC News, July 28, 2003; http://news.bbc.co.uk/2/hi/uk_news/england/manchester/3104839.stm.

2.   Alexis de Tocqueville, *Democracy in America*, (London: Penguin, 2003), 534, 713.

3.   Visit http://www.pbs.org/kcts/affluenza/.

4.   Tom Vanderbilt, "Self-storage Nation: Americans Are Storing More Stuff Than Ever," July 18, 2005; http://www.slate.com/id/2122832/.

5.   Mark J. Perry, "New US homes today are 1,000 square feet larger than in 1973 and living space per person has nearly doubled," American Enterprise Institute, June 5, 2016, http://www.aei.org/publication/new-us-homes-today-are-1000-square-feet-larger-than-in-1973-and-living-space-per-person-has-nearly-doubled/, accessed December 14, 2017.

6.   "Self Storage Industry Statistics," Statistic Brain, September 4, 2016, https://www.statisticbrain.com/self-storage-industry-statistics/, accessed December 14, 2017.

7.   Erin El Issa, "2017 American Household Credit Card Debt Study," NerdWallet, November 10, 2017, https://www.nerdwallet.com/blog/average-credit-card-debt-household/, accessed December 14, 2017.

8. Lindsay Konsko, "How Does My Credit Card Issuer Come Up With My Minimum Payment?," NerdWallet, April 1, 2014, https://www.nerdwallet.com/blog/credit-cards/credit-card-issuer -minimum-payment/, accessed December 14, 2017.

9. Dana Dratch, "Car Loans Keep Getting Longer," Bankrate, November 1, 2006, for; http://www.bankrate.com/brm/news /auto/20060815a1.asp.

10. Claire Ballentine and Jamie Butters, "U.S. Average Auto Loan Length Balloons to All-Time High," Bloomberg, July 5, 2017, https://www .bloomberg.com/news/articles/2017-07-05/u-s-average-auto-loan -length-balloons-to-all-time-high, accessed December 14, 2017.

11. Selena Maranjian, "Our National Savings Rate Is Embarrassing," The Motley Fool, January 17, 2007, ; www.fool.com/personal-finance /retirement/2007/01/17/our-national-savings-rate-is-embarrassing.aspx.

12. Matthew Frankel , "Here's the Average American's Savings Rate," The Motley Fool, October 3, 2016, https://www.fool.com/saving /2016/10/03/heres-the-average-americans-savings-rate.aspx, accessed December 14, 2017.

13. "A Look at the Shocking Student Loan Debt Statistics for 2017," Student Loan Hero, September 13, 2017, https://studentloanhero .com/student-loan-debt-statistics/, accessed December 14, 2017.

14. Bill Fay, "Managing Student Loan Debt," Debt.org, https://www.debt .org/students/debt/, accessed December 14, 2017.

15. Dave Ramsey, *Pricele$$* (Nashville: J. Countryman, 2002), 56.

16. Craig M. Gay, "Sensualists without Heart," *The Consuming Passion,* edited by Rodney Clapp (Downers Grove, IL: InterVarsity Press, 1998), 36.

Chapter 2: Wisdom and Finance

1. Todd Campbell, " The Shockingly Small Amount Americans Have in Retirement Savings," The Motley Fool, April 30, 2017, https://www. fool.com/retirement/2017/04/30/the-shockingly-small-amount-that-americans-have-in.aspx, accessed December 14, 2017.

2.   Magali Rheault, "Statistics About Eating Dinner Out," *Kiplinger's Personal Finance Magazine*, October 2000, http://findarticles.com /p/articles/mi_m1318/ is_10_54/ai_65368848.

3.   George Bernard Shaw, *Man and Superman* (London: Penguin, 2001), 32.

4.   See story at www.barbaraglanz.com.

5.   Dave Ramsey, *The Total Money Makeover* (Nashville: Thomas Nelson, 2007), 102–108.

Chapter 3: Cultivating Contentment

1.   "What They Saved From the Fire" photo essay, *Time*, http://www. time .com/time/photogallery/0,29307,1675264 _1472476,00.html.

2.   See www.worldofquotes.com/author/James-Mackintosh/1/index.html.

3.   Recycling-Revolution.com statistics; http://www.recycling-revolution. com/ recycling-facts.html.

4.   John Maxwell popularized this way of framing the question, though it was first published in 1975 by Viola Walden in her *Sword Scrapbook II* (Sword of the Lord), 40.

Chapter 4: Defined by Generosity

1.   "A Covenant Prayer in the Wesleyan Tradition," in *The United Methodist Hymnal* (Nashville: The United Methodist Publishing House, 1989), 607.

2.   D. James Kennedy and Jerry Newcombe, *Lord of All: Developing a Christian World-and-Life View* (Wheaton, IL: Crossway Books, 2005), 274.

3.   Kerry A. Dolan, "Forbes 2017 Billionaires List: Meet The Richest People On The Planet," Forbes, March 20, 2017,https://www.forbes .com/sites/kerryadolan/2017/03/20/forbes-2017-billionaires-list-meet -the-richest-people-on-the-planet/#14ab3a3a62ff, accessed December 15, 2017.

Epilogue: Living the Good Life

1. Graeme Wood, "Secret Fears of the Super-Rich," *The Atlantic*, April 2011, https://www.theatlantic.com/magazine/archive/2011/04/secret-fears-of-the-super-rich/308419/, accessed December 15, 2017.

2. John Helliwell, Richard Layard and Jeffrey Sachs, eds., "World Happiness Report," (report, The Earth Institute: Columbia University, 2012, 43, http://www.earth.columbia.edu/sitefiles/file/Sachs%20 Writing/2012/World%20Happiness%20Report.pdf.

3. Sarah Vermunt, "Success vs. Happiness: Don't Be Fooled Into Thinking They're the Same," *Entrepreneur*, https://www.entrepreneur.com/article/243605, accessed December 15, 2017.

4. Helliwell, 96.

5. "Jrue Holiday Stats," ESPN, http://www.espn.com/nba/player/stats /_/id/3995/jrue-holiday, accessed December 15, 2017.

6. D'Arcy Maine, "Jrue Holiday reflects on wife Lauren's brain tumor and surgery in new video," ESPN, March 29, 2017, http://www.espn.com/espnw/culture/the-buzz/article/19031181/jrue-holiday-reflects-wife-lauren-brain-tumor-surgery-new-video, accessed December 15, 2017.

7. Clayborne Carson, ed., *The Autobiography of Martin Luther King, Jr.* (New York: IPM/Warner Books, 2001), 21.

8. William Miller, "Death of a Genius: His fourth dimension, time, overtakes Einstein, Subsection: Old Man's Advice to Youth: 'Never Lose a Holy Curiosity'," *Life*, published May 2, 1955, https://books.google.com/boks?id=dlYEAAAAMBAJ&q=%22man+of+value %22#v=onepage&q=Death%20of%20a%20genius&f=false , accessed December 15, 2017.

FORGIVENESS

A dam Hamilton equates our need to forgive with carrying a backpack filled with rocks. Over time the tiny pepples and giant boulders weigh us down and break more than our spirit. In *Forgiveness: Finding Peace Through Letting Go*, Hamilton shows readers how to receive the freedom that comes with forgiving—even if the person needing forgiveness is ourselves.

Read *Forgiveness* on your own or, for a more in-depth study, enjoy it with a small group

ISBN 978-1-5018-5849-9

"Adam Hamilton not only reminds us about the importance of reconnecting the broken pieces of our lives, but shows how the process of grace and forgiveness is possibly our most complete picture of God."

— **Shane Stanford**, author of *Making Life Matter*

Available wherever fine books are sold.

For more information about Adam Hamilton, visit www.AdamHamilton.org

WHY?

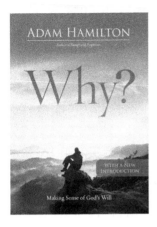

When the ground shakes, and a poor nation's economy is destroyed; when the waters rise, washing away a community's hopes and dreams; when a child suffers neglect and abuse; when violence tears apart nations: Where is God? In *Why? Making Sense of God's Will*, best-selling author Adam Hamilton brings fresh insight to the age-old question of how to understand the will of God. Rejecting simplistic answers and unexamined assumptions, Hamilton addresses how we can comprehend God's plan for the world and ourselves.

Read *Why?* on your own or, for a more in-depth study, enjoy it with a small group.

ISBN 978-1-5018-5828-4

"I recommend this book to anyone who longs to leave behind simplistic answers and discover a God who invites them into a collaborative process of bringing redemption, love, and hope to a world in desperate need."

—**Lynne Hybels**, author of *Nice Girls Don't Change the World*

Available wherever fine books are sold.

For more information about Adam Hamilton, visit www.AdamHamilton.org

CPSIA information can be obtained
at www.ICGtesting.com
Printed in the USA
LVHW08s1948181018
593702LV00004B/1/P

9 781501 857881